Voices in the Hall

Echoes of Students Past and Present

Education Advisors

Candice Fung
Teacher/Curriculum Leader English and Drama
Lambton Kent District School Board
Chatham, ON

Irene Heffel
Literacy Consultant
Edmonton Public School Board
Edmonton, AB

Patricia Mountain
Secondary English Teacher
North Vancouver School District 44
North Vancouver, BC

Reviewers

Sabrina Armstrong
Student Success Literacy Coach
Durham District School Board, ON

Dave Ellison
Humanities Teacher
Surrey School District 36, BC

Sonia Mangieri
AISI Content Literacy Consultant, Grades 7–10
Edmonton Catholic Schools, AB

Bryan J. Smith and Students
Department Head English and Media
Thames Valley District School Board, ON

Natalie Strecker
EAL and ELA Teacher
Winnipeg School Division, MB

McGraw-Hill Ryerson

Toronto   Montréal   Boston   Burr Ridge, IL   Dubuque, IA
Madison, WI   New York   San Francisco   St. Louis   Bangkok
Bogotá   Caracas   Kuala Lumpur   Lisbon   London   Madrid
Mexico City   Milan   New Delhi   Santiago   Seoul
Singapore   Sydney   Taipei

COPIES OF THIS BOOK
MAY BE OBTAINED BY
CONTACTING:

McGraw-Hill Ryerson Ltd.

WEB SITE:
http://www.mcgrawhill.ca

E-MAIL:
orders@mcgrawhill.ca

TOLL-FREE FAX:
1-800-463-5885

TOLL-FREE CALL:
1-800-565-5758

OR BY MAILING YOUR
ORDER TO:
McGraw-Hill Ryerson
Order Department
300 Water Street
Whitby, ON L1N 9B6

Please quote the ISBN and
title when placing your order.

McGraw-Hill Ryerson
Voices in the Hall: Echoes of Students Past and Present

ISBN 13: 978-0-07-106692-1
ISBN 10: 0-07-106692-6

http://www.mcgrawhill.ca

1 2 3 4 5 6 7 8 9   TCP   1 9 8 7 6 5 4 3 2

Printed and bound in Canada

PUBLISHER: Sandra McTavish
SENIOR CONTENT MANAGER: Rivka Cranley
SENIOR DEVELOPMENTAL EDITOR: Tracey MacDonald
DEVELOPMENTAL EDITOR: Megan Robinson
ACQUISITIONS EDITOR: Emily Pohl-Weary
MANAGER, EDITORIAL SERVICES: Crystal Shortt
SUPERVISING EDITOR: Jeanette McCurdy
COPY EDITOR: Karen Rolfe
REVIEW COORDINATORS: Melanie Berthier, Jennifer Keay
EDITORIAL ASSISTANT: Erin Hartley
MANAGER, PRODUCTION SERVICES: Yolanda Pigden
PRODUCTION COORDINATOR: Tammy Mavroudi
ART DIRECTION: Jodie Bernard, Lightbox Visual Communications Inc.
ELECTRONIC PAGE MAKE-UP: Laserwords Private Ltd.
PHOTO RESEARCH: Jodie Bernard, Lightbox Visual Communications Inc.
PERMISSIONS: Danny Meldung, Photo Affairs, Inc.
COVER DESIGN: Jodie Bernard, Lightbox Visual Communications Inc.
COVER IMAGE: Françoise Nielly

About the Education Advisors

Candice Fung

Candice Fung lives in Chatham, Ontario, with her husband and two children. She is a curriculum leader of English and Drama at Chatham Kent Secondary School, where she teaches English. Candice has a Master of Education in Curriculum Studies from the University of Western Ontario. Her studies focused on issues of race, class, and gender in education, and her professional focus is engaging students in the possibilities literature has to offer.

Irene Heffel

Irene Heffel is a literacy consultant with Edmonton Public Schools. She is a highly respected educator with over thirty years of experience at all levels. She has worked with both elementary and secondary teachers to implement literacy across curriculum, assessment, data analysis, critical thinking, and oral language models. She has been involved with Alberta curriculum development and has helped staff to implement the elements of backward design as an effective planning tool to foster student engagement.

Irene lives with her husband Brian and son Nicholas in Edmonton, Alberta. She would like to thank these two most precious people for their ongoing support and never-ending faith in her.

Patricia Mountain

Patricia Mountain has been a secondary English teacher in the North Vancouver School District since 1994. She is accomplished in diversified instruction, curricular integration, and alternative assessment. Her diverse teaching experience includes Learning Assistance, remedial English, ESL, and English 12 Advanced Placement. Patricia earned a Master of Education and Technology from Simon Fraser University where her research focused on global education and critical media literacy. With forays into high-tech management, Patricia is also an experienced e-learning writer, consultant, and blogger. She does seventeen loads of laundry each week and can hardly wait for her three daughters to learn how to drive.

iLit Series Contributors

iLit Series Education Advisors

Dr. Geraldine Balzer
University of Saskatchewan, SK

Cathy Coelho
Dufferin-Peel Catholic District School Board, ON

Rachel Cooke
Toronto District School Board, ON

Mary Curk
Thames Valley District School Board, ON

Eryn Decoste
Toronto District School Board, ON

Danielle Desjardins-Koloff
Windsor Essex-Catholic District School Board, ON

Donna Giacalone-Miller
Hamilton-Wentworth Catholic District School Board, ON

Starleigh Grass
Gold Trail School District 74, BC

Michael Halfin
York Region District School Board, ON

Lyanda Jackson
Dufferin-Peel Catholic District School Board, ON

Janet Kish
Toronto District School Board, ON

Katherine Kristalovich
Winnipeg School Division, MB

Lisa Loughlin
Toronto Catholic District School Board, ON

Dr. Janet E. McIntosh
Nipissing University, ON

Rachel A. Mishenene
Matawa First Nations Education Department, ON

Siobhan Mulroy
Near North District School Board, ON

Sue Schleppe
Maple Ridge & Pitt Meadows School District 42, BC

Bryan J. Smith
Thames Valley District School Board, ON

Dr. Pamela Rose Toulouse
Laurentian University, ON

Ann Varty
Trillium Lakelands District School Board, ON

Alex White
Calgary District School Board, AB

Melanie White
Ottawa-Carleton District School Board, ON

Ken Whytock
Waterloo Region District School Board, ON

iLit Series Reviewers

Table of Contents

Table of Contents

1

Visual Forms

BIG IDEA >

How do artists and authors use visual forms to project, or represent, themselves?

What are visual forms?

Visual forms use images to communicate. Text forms (such as short stories, poems, and essays) rely on words to convey meaning, whereas visual forms rely on symbols such as shape, colour, size, and sometimes words to convey meaning. In this section, you will find a range of visual forms from graphic stories about teen life, to an illustrated horror movie survival guide, to graffiti found in the halls of a high school.

How do I read visual forms?

> **Use visual literacy skills**—Ask yourself why an artist intentionally chose particular colours, shapes, sizes, and symbols. Consider the differences and similarities in the way visual and text forms speak to us.

> **Think about how words add to the visual message**—In some selections, words may be an essential part of the artwork and work with the images to tell a story or make a statement. In other selections, words may help to clarify the artist's intentions or explain the meaning of the artwork.

SCARY MOVIE SURVIVAL GUIDE

Illustrated Guide

Written by Mariko Tamaki

Illustrated by Steven Keewatin Sanderson

Mariko Tamaki's writing and performing career began during her university days in Montreal. Since then, she has moved from performing open-mic poetry to a career in writing that includes theatre, film, comics, and novels. Mariko's upcoming books include a novel, *(You) Set Me on Fire*, and a comic with Jillian Tamaki, *Awago Beach Babies*.

Tips

scenario: an outline or model of an imagined sequence of events

rhetorical question: a question for which no answer is expected

genre: category or type of literary work or entertainment; for example, horror movies

forward slash [/]: a punctuation mark most commonly used as a substitute for the word *or*. The author uses forward slashes in this selection several times, for example "eradication/extinction/execution" and "house/room/hotel"

Before

Preview the selection. Look at the headings and describe how the author organized her "survival guide."

During

Many words appear in all capital letters (ALL CAPS) in this selection. As you read, think about why the author chose to use ALL CAPS in each instance. Record your ideas on sticky notes.

Ever had a friend turn zombie in front of your very eyes? Witnessed an alien attack? Noticed a dark figure lurking in the hotel lobby?

If you are a fan of horror films, you know that any of these scenarios can lead to a person's eradication/extinction/execution. The question is, What have you learned from watching horror movies about how to survive in this world?

Drawing on her experience with the horror genre, Mariko Tamaki proposes a series of common-sense tips for people who want to avoid being a bloody bit part in the real-life fictional world of possible horrors.

SCENARIO 1:

See: *28 Days Later, 30 Days of Night, Dawn of the Dead*

It's Sunday afternoon. You're hanging with your friends, when you're interrupted by a news flash.

A virus is turning everyday people into people eaters.

What do you do?

First, let's be clear what you're up against: a force of rabid creatures that will be (a) everywhere and (b) out to eat you (and possibly make you one of them). It's peer pressure of the worst kind.

As a result of their pure protein (a.k.a. FLESH) diet, carnivorous zombies are running machines. You cannot outrun them. What you need is not an escape route, but a hideout plan.

Of which there are two:

1. LEAVE TOWN. Get all your most important possessions. Grab some canned goods. Pack some weapons, load your car with extra gas, and hit the road. Drive until you're far away from the populace of monsters.

Problem: Cars always need more gas. Somehow, zombies know this and so frequently target gas stations. Alternately, they'll get you while you sit in traffic waiting to get on the expressway.

2. FIND A BUNKER. Gather food and water and hide out in the city, either inside a mall or gym or any place that is not on floor level and all windows.

Problem: You will eventually have to leave your bunker for more canned goods or a decent magazine. Outside your bunker, you are easy pickings. (I still think the bunker is the better option, because you could hide out in the mall and that, at least, would be more fun than being stuck in a car.)

Final words: Stock up. Survive.

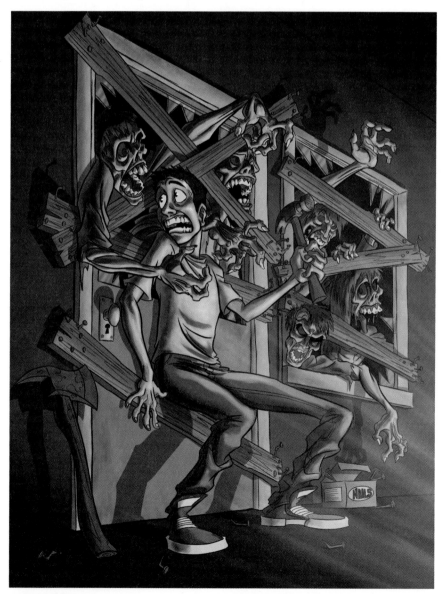

SCENARIO 2:

See: *Paranormal Activity, 1408, Poltergeist, The Amityville Horror, The Others, The Changeling*

You're spending the night in your creepy Great Aunt Edna's house. Everything seems fine until the stroke of midnight, when you notice ghosts smearing blood on the walls in the dining room.

What do you do?

Here's the thing about ghosts and horror movies that defies reason. Future victims ALWAYS know that the house/room/hotel they're about to enter is haunted. There is ALWAYS a warning, something like "several magicians were murdered in the attic" or even "every family that's ever lived here has gone insane."

Why don't people take these warnings to heart?

Because they don't believe. More than that, they're willing to stay in a haunted place to prove that paranormal stuff isn't real.

Why?

No one is handing out cash prizes to anyone who can prove such a thing. And you know what they're handing out to people who stay in haunted places and get attacked by ghosts? Body bags.

So, first rule: If you know a house is haunted, DON'T STAY THERE.

Second rule: Don't buy things that look like they might be important to a ghost, such as old rings or books or amulets.

Third: As soon as you find out a house is haunted, and furniture starts moving around, or mysterious writing appears on the walls, LEAVE. If you own the house, sell it.

Final words: Avoid creepy haunted places at all costs. And be nice to ghosts.

SCENARIO 3:

See: *Alien* (all), *Predator* (all), *Signs, Independence Day, War of the Worlds, Cloverfield*

It's a lazy Saturday afternoon. You're hanging with your friends, eating pizza and talking about how much you hate Physics (or Geography or English), when, suddenly, you're interrupted by a news flash: Aliens Are Invading!

Typically, ships hover over major cities, so maybe a ship's been spotted hovering over New York or Toronto. Maybe it's Calgary.

What do you do?

First, DON'T be curious. The curious are the first to get liquidated. And definitely don't approach the aliens with peace offerings. You will almost certainly get zapped doing this.

Okay, maybe the aliens have arrived with the best of intentions. If this is the case, the alien landing will be followed by a series of meetings between government officials and alien leaders, which will eventually be broadcast on TV.

If this is not the case, and it's probably not, you need to get out of town. Bunkers are not an option. Aliens, unlike zombies, can locate underground hideouts. They can also just vaporize the entire city where your bunker is located. However, aliens are very unlikely, it seems, to vaporize small country towns, so that's where you should head. Immediately.

Final words: Stock up. Leave town. Hope for the best.

SCENARIO 4:

See: *Orphan, The Omen, Children of the Corn, Case 39, The Ring, Rosemary's Baby*

Your new best friend, John, is a regular kid. Except that everyone who's even remotely mean to him ends up meeting some sort of mysterious demise.

Oh. Wait. Whoops.

Evildoers in movies, *serious* evildoers, exist as lessons in the dangers of prejudging. People think they can spot an evildoer, but they're often dead wrong. The *evil kid* is not the Goth playing Magic Cards at recess. What do evildoers need with Magic Cards? Evildoers play real-life Magic Cards. They play Magic Cards with people's souls!

Evildoers look ordinary. They look like kids who play team sports. They look just like happy "regular" boys and girls, but when you turn your back, they set your house on fire with their eyes.

If you are worried about accidentally befriending someone who is evil, note that evildoers rarely want friends; they want followers, key to the creation of an evil empire. If someone wants to be your friend, and is willing to play Wii when you want to play Wii, you should be good. If your new friend always insists you do what he or she wants, is unwilling to compromise, or threatens to turn you into a worm if you don't co-operate, then that, my friend, is an evildoer.

Unfriend this person immediately.

Final points: Keep your eyes peeled. Be a friend and not a follower.

What Inspired Me to Write This Selection

> Some people like to have pie after they watch a movie. For me, a good movie is made better if it can be followed by a lengthy debate. Horror movies provide the richest inspiration for argument because they're all about good people making bad choices: trusting the wrong people, taking the wrong turn, picking the wrong sleepover camp, and so on. The question is, hypothetically, what would YOU, if you are so smart, do DIFFERENTLY (in order to avoid being—say—eaten)? This piece was inspired by the ongoing debate I have with my friend Carolyn about the best way to escape a zombie attack, which essentially boils down to an urban versus rural argument (mall versus cabin in the woods). Carolyn says woods, I say mall. Carolyn is wrong.

After

1. **Understanding Form and Style**   Why do you think the author started her "survival guide" with rhetorical questions? Was this an effective introduction for you, the reader? Explain.

2. **Reading for Meaning**   In Scenario 4, the author says, "Evildoers in movies, *serious* evildoers, exist as lessons in the dangers of prejudging." What can you infer the author means about prejudging people?

3. **Student Voice**   Write a letter to the author responding to her advice in one of the scenarios. Do you agree or disagree with her advice? Do you have suggestions to add?

4. **Understanding Form and Style**   How do you know this "survival guide" is supposed to be humorous instead of serious? Provide examples from the text and art to support your answer.

5. **Speaking and Listening**   Choose one of the four scenarios from this selection. In a small group, dramatize someone carrying out the author's advice for that scenario. Try to mimic the author's sense of humour in your dramatization.

6. **Critical Literacy**   What do you think the author's attitude is towards horror movies and their viewers? How do you know?

7. **Metacognition**   How might paying attention to how the author created humour in this selection help you create humour in your own writing?

Beyond

Viewing and Representing   Imagine one of the four scenarios from the zombie/ghost/alien/evildoer point of view. Then create a guidebook with simple illustrations and instructions on how to attack and win. Consider using the advice given in this selection to help your characters succeed.

SOCIAL STATEMENT STENCILS

Graffiti

By Jessie Huggard, Megan Potts, Brooke Carey, and Courtney Morey

Tips

graffiti: writing or images painted onto public spaces

symbolism: the use of symbols to represent ideas or emotions

matrix: a graphic representation of information that includes symbols, numbers, and text. A matrix has two lines that intersect in the middle. Opposite ideas, such as survival and death, appear at each end of each line.

Before

As the saying goes, a picture is worth a thousand words. In what ways can images sometimes be more powerful than words?

During

As you look at each stencil and read the artists' explanations, write down one connected idea that comes to mind. For example, have you read a book or seen a movie about this topic? Does this remind you of another issue?

The Class Assignment

The social statement stencil project challenged students to make a statement about something that matters to them. The students were told that "if you could say one thing to everyone in the school, leave one mark on the walls for all to see, what would that statement be?"

Students researched various social issues and topics that interested them to find imagery and statistics to draw upon. The interesting thing about this particular project was the introspection it brought to the students. They may have started out with a flippant idea or joke, but as the project progressed, and they saw each other's statements evolving, suddenly what they were going to say took on much greater importance and meaning. Several students started over and over, revising their idea, not settling for the first thing that came to mind. In the end, they were very pleased with their results.

Each statement was created with Illustrator and Photoshop software; students sourced images from the Internet and repurposed them for their stencil. They had to think graphically because of the stark positive and negative space created by stencils. This forced students to create a clean image that would communicate their thoughts quickly and accurately, much like a logo. When placed in the stairway, the stencils would act as billboards. Students had to ensure the image and words would be understood quickly with no room for misinterpretation on the part of the passing reader.

—Stephen Morton
Media Arts, Visual Arts, and Photography Teacher
Huntsville High School

Stephen Morton's class in the stairway at Huntsville High School, where the students' stencils appear.

By Jessie Huggard

"I made the graffiti stencil 'Feel cool now?' to encourage people to take into consideration the lives of others when they drink and drive. Nobody seems to care anymore; all that's on their mind is their own selfish desires. I thought it would be helpful to show them the consequences of their actions ahead of time, so they can decide: is it worth it?"

By Megan Potts

"I chose this theme for my stencil to raise awareness of the kinds of relationships in today's society. I feel that a lot of girls are judged on their physical appearance, and can often be treated like a piece of meat. This is why I decided to have my stencil clearly state the difference: that women are not pieces of meat and that they should be treated with more respect. I think it is important to get to know someone for who they really are before you judge them."

" I chose to do my wall message about gay pride because of one of my favourite cousins. He is now openly gay, but when he was in high school he hid it, and had an absolutely miserable time. I don't think that people should have to hide who they are, because if you can't be yourself, it's really hard to be happy. I think that everyone deserves to be happy, no matter what sexual orientation they have. Being gay or straight is something that is part of you, and nobody should ever have to hide any part of him- or herself in order to be accepted by society. "

By Courtney Morey

" I chose this particular social statement because at least two of five people know women who have been abused or been in an abusive relationship. Those women lose all hope with every hit or punch because they're too afraid to leave the relationship and stand up to the person who is causing them so much pain. My social statement uses the pun, 'You don't have to wear a tank top to be a wife beater,' which plays on the white tank top known as a 'wife beater.' Anyone, even the most unlikely looking person, can be abusive towards another person. The reason I chose this statement is because I've had friends and family members who have gone through this, and it's not something anyone deserves for any reason. There is no excuse for this behaviour that continues to ruin many lives. "

After

1. **Reading for Meaning** Choose an image from each of the four stencils and explain how the image symbolizes an idea. For example, a skull and crossbones might symbolize death.

2. **Reading for Meaning** These stencils are intended to convey meaning quickly to people who walk by them. Answer the following questions to analyze the word choice for each stencil and infer meaning.
   a) Why would some people think drinking and driving is "cool"?
   b) What is meant by treating a girl "like a piece of meat"?
   c) What does the artist mean by "rainbows" and "in closets"?
   d) Why is a tank top sometimes unfairly called a "wife-beater"?

3. **Understanding Form and Style** In contrast to a longer text, how does the stencil format limit communication? How does the stencil format enhance communication? Use a chart like the one below to organize your ideas.

How Stencils Limit Communication	How Stencils Help Communication

4. **Student Voice** These stencils are a form of graffiti. In a persuasive paragraph, argue whether or not they are an appropriate and effective means of communication in school hallways.

5. **Critical Literacy** These students knew that their artwork would appear in the halls of their school. Do you think this knowledge affected the students' choice of messages and the way they presented their messages? Why or why not?

6. **Metacognition** Do you find the stencils easy or hard to understand? What features make them easy or hard to understand?

Beyond

1. **Reading for Meaning** Research one of the issues explored in the stencils. What causes, solutions, and data can you find about this issue? Present or display your findings in one of the following formats: an oral presentation, a magazine article, a matrix, or another graphical display.

2. **Viewing and Representing** If you could say one thing to everyone in your school, what would that statement be? Create a social statement stencil about an issue that is important to you.

Nowhere at Home

Graphic Story

Written by Claudia Dávila

Claudia Dávila was born in Chile and grew up in Montreal. She loves creating things, whether it's drawing, writing, making books and comics, or cooking, sewing and growing a garden. Her latest creation is the new graphic novel series *The Future According to Luz*.

Tips

panel: a framed section of a graphic story

speech bubble: a shape drawn around dialogue with a pointer towards the speaker

narrative box: a box in a panel that includes text that is not dialogue

Before

What emotions might be connected to feeling "nowhere at home"? Scan the panels and make a prediction about why the main character might feel this way.

During

As you read this selection, be sure to "read" the graphics as well as the text. If you need clarification, go back to previous panels to help you understand both the graphics and text.

What Inspired Me to Write This Selection

"
'Nowhere at Home' emerged from personal observations and experiences with visibly—and invisibly—different groups of people. My high school had diverse cultural groups and ethnicities, but everyone seemed to make fun of everyone else. To me, this seemed to limit individuals' freedom to discover and express their uniqueness, since others would notice only their most obvious difference. The flipside of this discrimination was that some people looked Caucasian but belonged to a different culture. My family is Chilean, yet no one would notice our difference. Discrimination shoeboxes people into one-sided identities and labels silence them. By appreciating people's unique characteristics, our understanding of one another can be more complex, enriched, and rewarding to everyone.
"

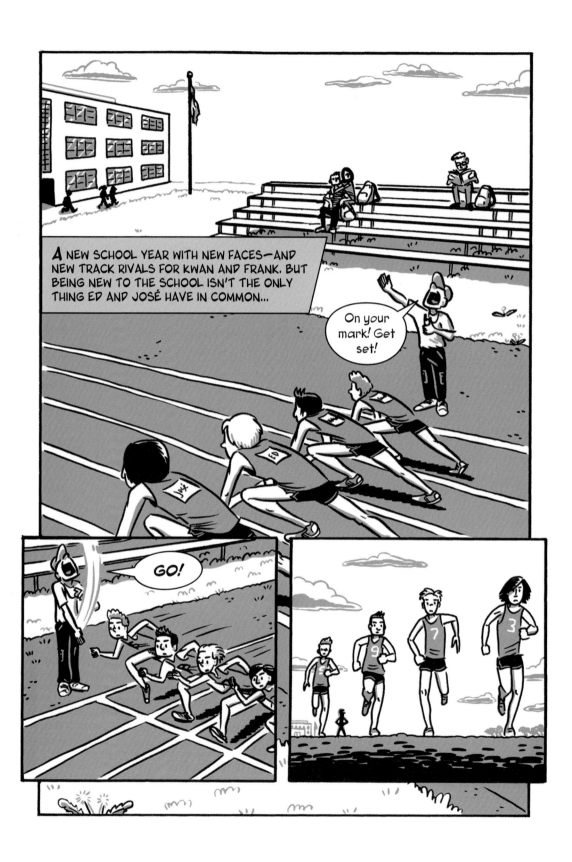

WELCOMED WARMLY BY HIS MOM, ED IS GREETED WITH HIS DAD'S USUAL ATTITUDE.

Hola, Eddy.

Hi, Mom.

Tsk! You'll never get better at Spanish if you only speak English, chico.

Sí, Papá.

Are you hungry?

How was the track meet?

Did you make new friends?

I came in second! Faster than Kwan, but this other guy José beat me by a hair.

José and Kwan?

Heh-hey! Los dos Latinos conquered el Chino!

Dad!

What the heck? Who cares if we're Latino?

And Kwan isn't Chino. He's Korean, okay?

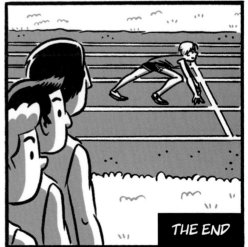

After

1. **Reading for Meaning** Why does Ed feel "nowhere at home"?

2. **Reading for Meaning** Why does it bother Ed that José is being teased for being Mexican? Choose the best answer below.
   A. Ed wishes he would get the kind of the attention that José is getting.
   B. Ed is Latino and he is afraid he would be stereotyped like José.
   C. Ed doesn't think José is Mexican.
   D. Ed wants to appear kind to impress his new friends.

3. **Understanding Form and Style** Reread all the narrative boxes in this graphic story.
   a) What is the purpose of the narrative boxes?
   b) Are some of the narrative boxes more important than others? Explain.

4. **Viewing and Representing**
   a) Look at the images in this graphic story and describe how the author portrayed movement and emotions.
   b) Consider what the story would be like without these visual effects. Do you think the visual effects are important to the story? Why or why not?

5. **Student Voice**
   a) Why do you think many high school students want to feel like they belong, or fit in?
   b) What factors do you think contribute to a sense of belonging?

6. **Critical Literacy**
   a) What is the author's main message?
   b) Why do you think the author wanted to write a story with this message?

7. **Metacognition** What strategies did you use to try to clarify anything you didn't understand in this story? Were these strategies helpful? Why or why not?

Beyond

Creating Media Texts Create a media text that promotes respect for other cultures. It could be in the form of a commercial on TV, an ad in a magazine, or a Web page. Share your media text with a classmate and get his or her feedback on how to improve it. Make sure to check your text for spelling and grammar errors.

PORTRAITS

Artwork

By Karmen Fofana, David Clifton, and Gabby Krizan

Before

This selection involves paintings, explanations of those paintings, and short biographies of the student artists who painted them. View and read this selection with the goal of making connections between what each artist says and how he or she represents those ideas and emotions visually.

During

For each portrait, write one question you have about the meaning of the picture.

Tips

portrait: a likeness of a person, particularly showing the face, created by an artist or photographer

self-portrait: a portrait an artist has created of him- or herself

archetype: typical or perfect example of something; for example, "They are the *archetype* of a modern family."

symbolism: the use of symbols to represent ideas or emotions; for example, in the portrait *The Seeker*, the bird is a symbol of freedom

The Seeker

By Karmen Fofana

Karmen Fofana emigrated from Liberia with his parents and brother. When he started elementary school in Canada, he got his name Karmen. His real name is Karmoh, but people were not pronouncing it right, so he changed it to Karmen. To him, it sounded better and also made him feel like a new person. He explains how his interest in art began: "I had a friend named Faki who was good at drawing anime characters and he usually got the most attention in class. I wanted to get attention too, so I started watching anime and practising how to draw them. One day I did a sketch that was better than Faki's and I started getting attention in class! The next day Faki brought a sketch that was better than mine, and from there, we started competing." Karmen currently attends Eastwood Collegiate Institute.

> I chose the title *The Seeker* because I consider myself a seeker. I painted myself a little older than I am now. I am holding a ball of light and energy, which is to help me find my way in life. On the right side, I have a painted a woman wearing a butterfly mask to make her mysterious; she symbolizes hope. Above the woman is a golden bird, which symbolizes freedom and strength. Above me there is an apple, which symbolizes all that I seek in life. On the left side of the apple, I painted God's arms coming out of space. One arm is on my shoulder and it is pointing out to the real world, and the other arm is trying to grab the apple. On the left side of me, I painted different coloured lines that connect, which symbolize all of my friends and different people who I have met in my life.

SELF-PORTRAIT

By David Clifton

David Clifton was born in Canada. His mother is from South Korea, and his father was born in Canada to parents who emigrated from England. This mix of cultures has been a lifelong lesson of acceptance and tradition for David. His interests include visual arts, music, writing, and martial arts. He currently attends Eastwood Collegiate Institute in the Integrated Arts program. David plans on attending university or college to pursue either a fine arts or illustration degree.

> The project is a self-portrait, in which I portrayed myself as the archetype of artist. The media I used are graphite, Conté, acrylic paint, and modelling paste. The montage of hands and faces represents the most important tools of an artist and the range of emotions an artist can portray, such as calm, happy, sad, intense, and so on. I also included an image of myself playing guitar, showing the variety in my artistic expression. The lines and shadows fade into space and into each other, symbolizing the way ideas and emotions can change. This work represents an acceptance of identity and the artist's journey.

Sweeney

By Gabby Krizan

Gabby Krizan was born in Livno, Bosnia. She immigrated to Canada at the age of two and grew up in Kitchener, Ontario. She currently attends Eastwood Collegiate Institute as an Integrated Arts program student and aspires to be an illustrator/graphic designer. Gabby enjoys working in a variety of media from painting and drawing to sculpture and digital artwork. Her artwork was featured in Embark, a senior graduating art exhibition at a local gallery. She was also the chief editor and designer of the catalogue for this exhibition.

" *Sweeney* is a digital painting rendered in Adobe Photoshop. It was hand drawn using a tablet. I painted the murderous barber Sweeney Todd, from the musical of the same name. I tried to capture a sense of the gritty personality of the main character. I overlaid various textures in the background and foreground to assist in denoting the character's persona: a sinister barber of industrial England. "

After

1. **Reading for Meaning**   How are the three portraits similar? How are they different? Use a Venn diagram to record your ideas.

2. **Reading for Meaning**   For each portrait, write one or two sentences to describe the picture.

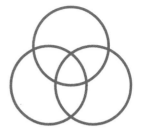

3. **Understanding Form and Style**   Choose one portrait and explain how the images in the paintings, including their colours, shapes, and sizes, convey symbolic meaning. Refer to the artists' explanations of their art for help.

4. **Speaking and Listening**   Discuss the portraits with a partner. Use the questions you wrote during reading to guide your discussion.

5. **Student Voice**   Which portrait most clearly communicates meaning to you? Why?

6. **Critical Literacy**
   a)   Do you think these portraits each represent the entire person? Why or why not?
   b)   What types of information about the people are not shown or communicated?

7. **Metacognition**
   a)   How did writing questions about the portraits help you discuss them with another student?
   b)   How did discussing with another student improve your understanding of the portraits?

Beyond

1. **Viewing and Representing**   Create a self-portrait in a format of your choice, such as a painting, computer-generated illustration, collage, or sculpture. Write a paragraph to explain how your self-portrait represents you.

2. **Viewing and Representing**   Find a self-portrait of a famous artist (for example, Picasso, Van Gogh, Frida Kahlo, Andy Warhol, etc.). Compare the self-portrait with a photograph of the artist. Research the artist's life to try to find out why the artist may have painted him- or herself this way. Present the portrait and your findings about it to your class.

THIS PICTURE REPRESENTS ME

Visual Representation

Written by Kenneth Sutherland

My name is Kenny and I was born in Vancouver. My biological family is Native, and my foster family is white. I was four months old when my foster mother got me. She raised me and many other children on her own. My foster mother is generous and caring. I always had anger problems, even as a child. That caused problems in school. I dropped out in Grade Nine, and then attended an alternative program, which I hated. I am currently at a great school called the North Surrey Learning Centre.

Tips

symbol: one thing that stands for another, as in a flag representing a country

bullet point: a word or short phrase with a small printed symbol in front of it. Bullet points are often used in lists or to set apart important points in a larger piece of writing.

infer: to understand something based on what the author states or implies as well as your prior knowledge or experience

Before

Read the title of this selection and look at the illustration. What do you predict the illustration is meant to show about the author? Why do you think this?

During

A lot of things are left unsaid in this selection. As you read, write at least three questions that you'd like to ask the author to better understand what he is saying or why he illustrates things the way he does.

This picture represents me, my three sisters, and our mother.

 • The purple line is my mother, who abandoned all of us (or at least me), leaving me addicted to alcohol and drugs.

 • The needle and thread represents her trying to be a part of my life and mending the past. Which I don't want. Won't happen.

 • The green/purple line is my sister with a different father.

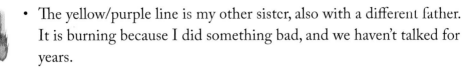

- The yellow/purple line is my other sister, also with a different father. It is burning because I did something bad, and we haven't talked for years.
- The red/purple line is my full-blood sister.
- The BIG purple/red line with inverted colors is me. The colors are opposite because I am different from them all.

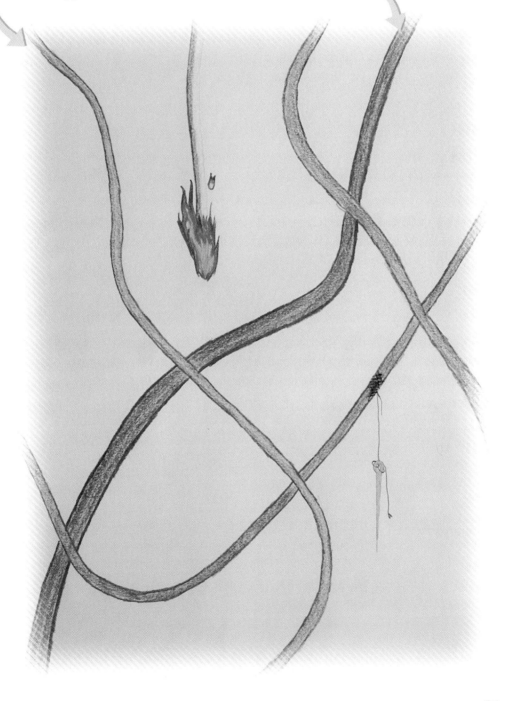

What Inspired Me to Create This Selection

" I am heavily influenced by music, and all my creative work is done while listening to metal. I did this abstract drawing in my art class when I was eager to use my new pencil crayons. It wasn't an assignment; I just wanted to experiment. I was listening to Kind Diamond, a metal band. The drawing started off as just curved lines going from one side of the page to another. As I soon as I did the fifth line, I knew why I was drawing them, and it progressed from there. I was encouraged to write an explanation about my drawing, and I'm glad I did, because I think the drawing is personal, but my words give it more power. Art and storytelling work together. I felt happy creating something other people can understand. "

After

1. **Reading for Meaning**   Before reading the selection, you made predictions about what it was about. Were your predictions correct? Explain.

2. **Reading for Meaning**   What can you infer about why the author doesn't want his mother in his life?

3. **Speaking and Listening**   If this author chose to represent his thoughts and feelings about his family as a short monologue, what would he say? Write and perform this monologue for someone, making sure to use what you feel would be the appropriate tone and facial expressions.

4. **Understanding Form and Style**   Why do you think the author chose to use bullet points in his explanation of his artwork? Do you think this was a good choice or would you have presented the text differently?

5. **Viewing and Representing**   The author used colours and symbols to represent his thoughts and feelings about his family. How effective were his choices? For example, if there was no written explanation included with this art, would you have been able to interpret any of these symbols and colours? Explain.

6. **Critical Literacy**   Why do you think the author created and published this selection? Why might he have wanted people to read it?

7. **Metacognition**
   a) In what ways did the text help you understand the illustration?
   b) In what ways did the illustration help you understand the text?

Beyond

Student Voice   Create an abstract piece of art (such as a computer-generated illustration, a hand-drawn illustration, or a photo collage) about your own family, or some other relationship. Use bullet points to explain your art.

OLD FRIENDS

Graphic Memoir

Written by Jillian Tamaki

Jillian Tamaki grew up in Calgary, Alberta, and currently lives in Brooklyn, New York. Her illustrations have won gold medals from the Society of Illustrators and the Society of Publication Designers. Jillian is the cocreator of the graphic novel *SKIM* (with Mariko Tamaki), which was listed as one of *The New York Times* Best Illustrated Books of 2008 and was nominated for four Eisner Awards and a Governor General's Literary Award.

Before

1. Preview this selection. Explain how you think the art and the text are meant to be read together. Why do you think that?
2. Before reading the text, predict what the text will reveal about the people in the art.

During

As you read this selection, be aware of which part you tend to look at first—the visuals or the text.

Tips

memoir: an account of the personal experiences of an author

sentence fragment: often looks like a sentence, but does not contain a complete thought because either the subject or predicate is missing or incomplete. The author uses sentence fragments throughout this selection; for example "Definitely the smartest boy. And nice, too."

What Inspired Me to Write This Selection

❝ The children in the stories are now adults, but in my mind, they'll always exist as ten, thirteen, or sixteen-year-olds. It's a little unfair, as I would most likely not want to be remembered as I was when I was that age—unformed and quite boorish. Oh well. It's amazing to think how these perfectly crystallized images (personal mythologies, really) must differ from the realities of the children's lives. Or reveal only a tiny bit of the "real story." At this point, these polished little stones of memory are more about myself, and less reflective of the individuals who originally inspired them. ❞

1. Kelly Flaherty sucked her three middle fingers well into elementary school. They were always dry and a bit withered from the abuse. Eventually her parents bribed her to give up the habit by buying her a bright yellow cassette tape player.

2. Helen Min and I were nest builders, tree doctors, petty thieves, horses, and hamburgers. She was braver and more co-ordinated than I was, and could stand on swings and do the monkey bars. My strengths were in naming our invented games and designing backyard obstacle courses. As an added bonus, her parents owned a Mac's convenience store, so we got free Coke Slurpees and frequent viewings of a cheesy movie about a dead rock 'n' roll singer (one of the few videos her store carried that was suitable for children).

3. Henry Joel Stevens was probably the smartest kid in Grade Six. Definitely the smartest boy. And nice, too. He had a very round head. Basically, he was Charlie Brown with more freckles.

4. Gretchen had very curly blond hair and a comically high voice, and played lead trombone in the school band. Despite all of that, she had successfully navigated her way to that tween-age social apex: The Back (and best) Seat on the Bus. She was a firm but kind alpha female who kept her small kingdom in check with judgmentally squinty eyes, rarely needing to resort to more extreme (or humiliating) tactics. I think we got along because I made her laugh, which, I have to say, felt fantastic.

5. Candy Flunn had a hilarious name and a bad attitude. In retrospect, I realize she probably had a really terrible home life. I'm not sure if knowing that about Candy would have made me feel sorry for her at the time. Mean.

6. Ana and I played *Girl Talk* in her bedroom and *Nightmare* in her family room, where their caged lovebird lived. Ana's dad developed M.S. when we were about eleven and wasted away very rapidly. I eventually stopped going over to their house.

7. Mike was an amputee and had a prosthetic arm. My mom babysat him at our place a few times. Once, at our kitchen table, under my mom's stained-glass hanging lamp, we cut out paper owls and coloured them

with pencil crayons. Mike always wore navy blue velour sweatpants. I had a tiny crush on him.

8. Katie was a woman by the time she was in Grade Five. Her mom was dead and she cried about it in class once when the teacher forced us to discuss "loss."

9. "Step on Brown, your pants fall down
Step on White, get a million dollars tonight."

10. Roxanne is one of the funniest people I have ever known. She was very deft at mocking others. She gave everyone creatively vague nicknames like "Brown Paper Bag Eyes." For some reason, people are surprised when I tell them that the funniest person I have ever known is a girl. Why?

11. I met Sarah in Grade Eight. Along with Roxanne, she spearheaded "Nerd Power," a two-person coalition dedicated to ironic buttons and flashcards, giving out "Winner" certificates and, perhaps most significantly, creating a series of jokes and riddles whose punch line was always "Nerds." I think I may have been an honourary member.

12. Children are the cruellest, most ruthless beings on earth. Everyone acknowledges this, but very few fess up to their own offences. Boys don't talk about beating up nerds, and girls pretend they never psychologically tormented others to the point of tears. We might admit to a few youthful misgivings, but generally pretend we were "good kids." The truth is really uncomfortable to admit. Impossible, maybe.

13. Tom was poor and everyone knew it. He also seemed kind of unlucky. Bad combination.

14. Faith Wotherspoon was one of those overachievers who harboured pure hatred for anyone whose ability, in any activity, approached her own. She also had a solid gold flute.

15. Rami was a raging dork* in elementary school, but by the time we entered high school, she had blossomed into a super-hot young woman with a great figure and a sexy, deep voice. That itself was reason enough to hate her, but the main source of our truly epic rivalry involved my offhand

comment that Michael Jackson was a "freak of nature." The fact this was even a source of drama is clear evidence that all Grade Ten girls are crazy.

16. Jemal liked romantic R&B "slow jams." And Rami.

17. Nora was the fairest of fair-weather friends. When you're ten, it's hard to resist the seduction of attention. In fact, knowing you'll be unfashionable again in a few days made it all the more delicious. The rumour at school was that Nora's dad went crazy. Apparently he was missing for a while and they found him sleeping on a beach in Florida.

18. Stephanie was from Montreal, and exuded sexiness in a way only Montreal girls can.

19. After years of disinterest, Hamid eventually took a Mormon girl to grad. That was probably the clearest sign I was going to get.

20. Ten-year-old Bryce Jennings had the shiniest, roundest of mushroom cuts and a really cool, neon-pink ski jacket. He was, in the simplest of terms, a dreamboat.

21. Samuel Hogarth is now a very famous soccer player living in Europe. He probably makes millions of dollars and lives a fabulously glamorous lifestyle. I think the girls could sense his potential because he was deemed crush-worthy. He used to make fun of my name. My mother unhelpfully suggested I call him "Samuel the Farmer" as a rebuttal.

22. Gina Gyzz had a horrible name and was an unabashed nerd, which takes guts in junior high. Daily torment didn't seem to affect her. Maybe she had a truly sunny disposition or maybe, by high school, she had perfected her coping mechanisms.

23. Maggie was a tattletale who couldn't take a joke. And she had horse teeth.

24. Goth kids are funny because they're just as dorky and awkward as your typical run-of-the-mill teenager. Behind closed doors, they cautiously pluck "Yesterday" on powder-blue Fender guitars and paint their bedroom walls with delightful cloud motifs. They have guilty pleasures like 1960s folk ballads and cheesy dance music. They make Betty Crocker instant cake mixes and lick batter off spoons. I've seen it.

After

1. **Reading for Meaning** Look back at the predictions you made before reading the text. Were your predictions correct? Explain.

2. **Understanding Form and Style** Think about what the selection would be like without the art. Then explain what purposes the art serves.

3. **Viewing and Representing** Choose three people in the art. Analyze the drawings and explain why you think the author represented these people the way she did.

4. **Critical Literacy** What does the text tell you about what the author values in people? Think about the people she seems to like and dislike. Support your answer with examples from the text.

5. **Critical Literacy** This is a memoir, which means the people the author is describing are real. Referring to the way she portrays people, the author says, "it's a little unfair, as I would most likely not want to be remembered as I was when I was that age—unformed and quite boorish."
   a) How might the people mentioned by the author react to this piece?
   b) How would you feel if someone wrote and published something like this about you?

6. **Student Voice** The author says, "Children are the cruellest, most ruthless beings on earth." Reread the rest of number 12. Decide whether you agree with the author. Explain why or why not.

7. **Metacognition** Think back to the During reading activity and whether you looked at the visuals or the text first when you read this selection.
   a) Think about why you were more drawn to the visuals or to the text. Do you usually find visuals or text easier to understand? Explain.
   b) How might knowing whether you usually find visuals or text easier to understand help you in this class as well as other classes?

Beyond

Student Voice In this selection, the author is looking back on friends she had in elementary and high school. Try the same thing. Think of two people you knew in elementary school. Write a journal entry or a letter, or a create artwork to express how you view them now.

JOHN JOSEPH, THE BOY WHOSE LAST NAME IS A FIRST NAME

Graphic Story

Written by Joe Ollmann

Born on a Christmas tree farm near Hamilton, Ontario, Joe Ollmann was raised by two nice parents with five older siblings. He now resides in Montreal, Quebec, drawing comics and wishing he had studied French more in school. Oh yeah—he also had his own pony when he was a kid.

Tips

panel: a framed section of a graphic story

narrative box: a box in a panel that includes text that is not dialogue; in this graphic story, the narrative boxes contain the thoughts of the main character, John Joseph

flashback: a literary device in which the plot is interrupted by an event or incident from an earlier time; the story goes back in time

caricature: an illustration or description of a person or thing in which certain qualities are exaggerated to create a comic effect

vocal inflection: changing the tone, pitch, or volume of your voice

Before

Brainstorm a list of similarities and differences between graphic stories (such as comics or graphic novels) and short stories.

During

In this graphic story, some panels show things that John Joseph is either remembering (as in a flashback) or imagining. As you read, pay attention to the stylistic clues—both in the illustrations and in the narrative boxes—to determine what type of scene you are viewing.

What Inspired Me to Write This Selection

> " The kind of awkward, embarrassing incident that happens to the main character in my story happened to me about a million times throughout my school career. To me, the most obvious story to write about high school would include an obsession about some girl who wouldn't know I existed and me doing some clumsy, idiotic thing in front of that girl. I would have never forgotten the embarrassment of an incident like that in those days. The nice thing about getting older is that you rarely get embarrassed about anything. "

JOHN JOSEPH, THE BOY WHOSE LAST NAME IS A FIRST NAME...

HOO!

...HE'S, UH—HE'S SORT OF A LOWER... LOWER-TO-MID-LEVEL, ACTUALLY, UH, A CLERK IN INSURANCE SALES...

BOOOOOORING!

...SPECIALIZING IN RISK MANAGEMENT, ACTUALLY...

OOOOH! RISK MANAGEMENT!!

HA HA

HA HA

HA HA

HA

HA

SETTLE DOWN, PEOPLE! ALBERT, WHAT DOES YOUR FATHER DO?

FATHERS' INCOMES BY PROFESSION

SOLDIER - III
CAR SALES - II
PILOT - I
MARTIAL - II
ARTIST
INSURANCE CLERK (RISK

MY DAD'S A CAPTAIN IN THE CANADIAN AIRFORCE. HE FLIES FIGHTER JETS.

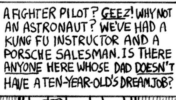

A FIGHTER PILOT? GEEZ! WHY NOT AN ASTRONAUT? WE'VE HAD A KUNG FU INSTRUCTOR AND A PORSCHE SALESMAN. IS THERE ANYONE HERE WHOSE DAD DOESN'T HAVE A TEN-YEAR-OLD'S DREAM JOB?

AND WHAT THE HELL DOES THIS HAVE TO DO WITH MATH? JUST ANOTHER WAY TO HUMILIATE ME IN FRONT OF THESE GORILLAS.

MY DAD SELLS INSURANCE, OKAY? IT'S NOT GLAMOROUS, BUT IF YOUR FACTORY BURNS DOWN, THE INSURANCE MAN IS YOUR BEST FRIEND.

AW MAN, I KNOW MY PARENTS ARE BORING AND THEY ARE SOOO MUCH OLDER THAN EVERYONE ELSE'S PARENTS. THE OTHER KIDS AND THEIR PARENTS PROBABLY SHARE PLAYLISTS ON THEIR MP3 PLAYERS.

AWESOME PLAYLIST, DAD!

HA HA

...MY DAD RUNS AN ONLINE DATING SERVICE...

OH, COME ON! WHAT IS IT WITH THAT JOCK-CLOWN, ANYWAY? IT'S NOT ENOUGH THAT HE LOOKS LIKE A GREEK GOD AND HAS "SPORTS SKILLS," HE HAS TO MOCK ME ALL THE TIME.

I LOVE MY PARENTS, BUT THEY ARE OLD AND BORING, AND I CONFESS I AM SOMETIMES EMBARRASSED BY THEM AND WISH THEY WOULD STAY AWAY FROM SCHOOL.

BUT THEY ARE DEDICATED AND TAKE ANY OPPORTUNITY TO SHOW UP UNANNOUNCED.

I'M MRS. JOSEPH, JOHN JOSEPH'S MOM...

...I HAVE HIS EPI-PEN KIT HERE. HE HAS A DEADLY PEANUT ALLERGY AND HE FORGOT HIS EPI-PEN TODAY!

EPI - PEN

After

1. **Reading for Meaning**
    a) It could be argued that John Joseph has a good sense of humour, but there are also things about his character that make him funny. Reread the story to find at least three humorous aspects of John Joseph's character.
    b) What qualities make John Joseph's character easy to relate to?

2. **Understanding Form and Style** Certain qualities of the parents, teachers, and students are exaggerated, both in the text and in the illustrations of this story. Describe three instances of this exaggeration. Explain the effect these caricatures have on you, the reader.

3. **Understanding Form and Style** How does the author symbolize John Joseph's peanut allergy?

4. **Speaking and Listening** With a partner, choose a page of this selection to read aloud. Pay attention to both graphic and language cues to guide your dramatic reading. Reflect these cues with your vocal inflection, facial expressions, and body language. Give feedback to each other on your readings.

5. **Viewing and Representing** Choose a panel where there is no text. Use inferencing to explain what is happening in that illustration.

6. **Student Voice** In this story, John Joseph uses his sense of humour as a coping mechanism for his problems, such as being made fun of in class, his peanut allergy, and his troubles with girls. Do you think humour is a good way to deal with certain problems? Why or why not?

7. **Critical Literacy** How would this story differ if it were told from the jock's point of view or from the girl's (Teresa's) point of view?

8. **Metacognition** Do you usually understand a story better when it has illustrations? Why or why not?

Beyond

Reading for Meaning Write the next scene in John Joseph's story using one of the following formats: additional graphic story panels, a script for a TV show, or a short story. Remember to proofread your text and correct any spelling or grammatical errors.

Fiction and Poetry

BIG IDEA ›

How do your own values and experiences affect the way you read fiction and poetry?

What are fiction and poetry?

Fiction is a type of literary work that tells stories about imaginary events and people. Poetry, on the other hand, is not easily defined. The poet William Wordsworth explained it as "the spontaneous overflow of powerful feelings." Leonard Cohen says, "poetry is just the evidence of life. If your life is burning well, poetry is just the ash."

When we approach a text, we read the same words, but we all bring different experiences, views, and interests to what we read. These differences are why our perception of stories and poems varies from person to person. In this section, you will be reading stories and poetry from both professional writers and student writers covering themes such as regret, youthful recklessness, and sacrifice.

How do I read fiction and poetry?

› **Use inferencing**—Often, to fully understand a story or poem, you need to make inferences or "read between the lines." To make inferences, combine your prior knowledge of the topic or your own experiences with what the author is directly stating or implying.

› **Use visualizing**—Use your everyday experience of the world around you to help you visualize what the author is describing. Pay attention to sensory details describing smell, sight, touch, sound, and taste.

Make 'Em Laugh

Written by David Silverberg

David Silverberg is a poet, promoter, event organizer, journalist, and editor. He helps run a regular poetry slam and was festival director for the 2011 Canadian Festival of Spoken Word. He has written a book of poetry called *Bags of Wires* and compiled the spoken-word anthology *Mic Check*.

Tips

spoken word: a form of poetry recited to an audience. These poems often comment on current social issues and are told from the first-person perspective.

imagery: the use of sensory details to evoke a mental image. Imagery appeals to any of the five senses: sight, sound, taste, touch, or smell.

Before

"It's better to regret something you did than something you didn't do." This quotation is from the spoken-word poem you are about to read. Think of a time when you regretted doing something or *not* doing something. Describe it and then explain your feelings about the decision you made.

During

As you read, be aware of the images the author is painting in your mind. Write down the thoughts and emotions these images evoke in you.

When you're a fat guy in high school
You have three choices …
Be a bully
Be silent
Be funny
I tackled this multiple-choicer quickly.
I didn't want to inspire violence
So I crossed off bully.
I enjoyed moments of silence
But biting my tongue always left a sour taste in my mouth.
So I chose C,

rollin with my rolls to the flabby path of
just wanna make 'em laugh.
I deflected attention away from man-boobs
by slinging sly comments to a hungry audience.

When life hands you lemon meringue thighs,
you chug the lemonade and burp the alphabet.
In Grade Ten, I was all jokes,
I wanted to crackle laughter from caf to gym
to long walk home.
I made friends because I smiled a lot.
And used my charmingly chunky body to
sway people to *my* side.
It was one of the most meaningful decisions
I ever made in my life.

But
all around me, I saw my fellow fat kids
face bullies who get kicks out of curb-stomping self-esteem.
You know these bullies, angry-mouthed storm clouds
who can't wait for their nails to clench into their palms.
And on the other side of their knuckles
were these timid heavily husky boys
enduring a bruising barrage of insults,
hourly, daily, weekly.
They ate their lunch in bathroom stalls.
They avoided eye contact.

But when I saw this ugliness, I froze.
I became just a chalk outline of opportunity.
Maybe I was afraid.
Maybe I really wanted these kids to face the violence
that could've swung my way at any moment.
These attacks burst before me
like pumpkins smashed by brainless boots.

Being powerless at sixteen is like having at a stroke at seventy ...
You see yourself weakening,
the fog of pain drenching your good sense,
eyes peppered with shock.
And then the horse blinders pop up.
All I could do in those schoolyards
was walk on,
forget about it,
turbo my waddle around eager fists.

One time, I saw Charles face the hailstorm of snowballs from four tough kids
with nothing better to do.
I jogged around his weeping body
as if it were a small fire I needed to avoid.

It was one of the worst decisions I ever made in my life.

See, *I* wanted to be the funny guy,
and I was.
But I also gave myself the nonrefundable gift of cowardice.
I *shadowed* away from my double-chinned brethren
who could've been me
with their heads locked between muscles
and tears trembling down cheeks.

So you might be asking:
what could I have done?
I'm no fighter, let's be honest,
the last time I swung my fist was against a punching bag at my friend's house
and even then, it kind of hurt my knuckles.

But I like to think that I could've done *something*
joined in solidarity with my big-boned brothers
even if it was just an anonymous word to a teacher or principal.

I've always believed
It's better to regret something you did

than something you didn't do.
But would I have regretted breaking the shins of bullies
so they couldn't stand up to fight back?

Instead of drowning in guilt, I am saying all of this
to implore those who have not seen the fat kicked out of kids
to realize what goes on beyond a teacher's radar.
There is only so much we can do—that's true
but if we don't take action
out of laziness
fear
ignorance
then we are victims that deserve bloody noses that never stop hemorrhaging.

I don't regret that I was a fat kid in high school
I only hope that someone could say the words
I swallowed without even tasting them.

What Inspired Me to Write This Selection

> I've always believed you have to write what you know. It's the first rule of honest writing. When I started performing poetry and conducting workshops in schools, I thought back to my days as a teenager. I recalled my fears, my masks, my behaviour. I explored my shift from a shy guy to a funny guy, and it was fascinating to recognize my transformation all those years later.
>
> I hope "Make 'Em Laugh" is relevant to any student who feels afraid to stand up for his or her brothers and sisters. Sometimes, poetry speaks for the voiceless.

After

1. Reading for Meaning

   a) What did the author regret *not* doing as a teen? What reasons did he give for his inaction?

   b) Explain how the author as an adult feels about his inaction as a teen, and how he is trying to make up for it.

2. Understanding Form and Style

   a) The author chose to use a spoken-word poetic form to tell his story. Why do you think he chose this form?

   b) Do you think this was the best form to choose? If so, explain why. If not, explain what would have been a better form.

3. Understanding Form and Style   Refer back to the notes you made for the During reading activity. Comment on the effectiveness of the author's use of imagery in this poem. Give specific examples to support your answer.

4. Speaking and Listening   The author intended his spoken-word poem to be read aloud. Read it out loud to yourself while paying attention to the line breaks. How does this poem sound in comparison to a short story read aloud?

5. Student Voice   The author wrote that when he saw a boy who had been attacked by bullies, he "jogged around his weeping body as if it were a small fire [he] needed to avoid." Write a letter to yourself explaining in detail what you hope you would do if faced with a similar situation.

6. Critical Literacy   Who does this author show bias against and bias in favour of in this poem? What does this bias say about the author's values?

7. Metacognition   In the Before reading activity you thought back to a time when you made a decision you later regretted. How did drawing on your previous life experiences help you to better understand this text?

Beyond

Creating Media Texts   It can be hard to stand up for something you believe in, especially if there could be negative consequences for doing so. Create an illustrated flyer, radio ad, or Web page that encourages other students your age to always do what they feel is right.

Out of the Ashes

Short Story

Written by Maureen McGowan

Maureen McGowan is the author of *Cinderella: Ninja Warrior, Sleeping Beauty: Vampire Slayer* and the young adult science fiction thriller series, The Dust Chronicles. Aside from books and writing, she's passionate about art, dance, films, fine handcrafted objects, and shoes. Growing up, she lived in Regina, Ottawa, Montreal, Toronto, Winnipeg, and Georgetown.

Tips

genre: types or categories of text recognized by form and/or style; for example, essay, article, short story, graphic novel, poem, science fiction novel, mystery novel

simile: a comparison made using the words *like* or *as*

mood: the atmosphere of a piece of writing that is meant to evoke a certain emotion or feeling from the reader

prologue: an introduction to a literary work, such as a play, autobiography, or novel. This selection is the prologue to a set of three related novels, called a trilogy.

Before

The world has become unlivable in this story about the future. Predict what might happen to our society in such a situation. Think about who would have power, and who would be likely to survive.

During

In this story, the author slowly provides details to reveal what is going on in the world and with the main character. As you read, write down at least three questions you have about the situation or the setting.

A shriek punctures the darkness below the bridge. Raising my hands to cover my ears, I crunch the envelope against my cheek, then immediately press the creased paper against my thigh in a feeble attempt to hide the damage. High above, a streetlamp illuminates the thick air and I yearn towards the brightness, teasing me with its illusion of safety. There's no electricity in our part of the city and I'm starting to believe the doomsday theorists. It's been weeks since I could differentiate night and day, months since I've been bathed in this much light.

"Keep moving." A policeman stomps towards me, his head haloed by the light's glow, the ash floating above him like we're deep in an ocean of dust.

Squinting, I seek out his eyes, searching for kindness, some hint of humanity, but his dark shield and heavy mask engulf his face and demean the paper and elastic of my air filter. Designed for construction workers, my mask barely strains the ash, but at least it covers my nose and mouth, at least I've got something. At least I'm still alive, haven't drowned, haven't choked on the foul air—haven't changed.

And beyond that, I'm lucky. I was chosen to live in the dome they're calling Haven. Not that it came as a shock. My resumé was awesome, I aced my interview, was top of my class, got scholarships to all the top universities. I've always been an overachiever. Still …

"Stay away from the railings." The cop smacks his long gun against a heavy glove, then strides away from me to face the danger grasping toward us from below. For months, the police have been in full riot gear 24/7—freaky. I relax slightly now that he's gone.

I hadn't realized I'd veered so close to the edge, certainly didn't mean to, but after the cop's warning, the fence pulls me like a magnet. Disobeying his order, I step up onto the sidewalk to look down, where spotlights bomb the valley with circles of light—flashes of horror with a scream-filled soundtrack.

I glance back at my mom and brother behind me in the line of new hires trudging down the middle of the bridge then continue along the sidewalk, scanning below, horrified yet unable to look away. I knew the army had herded them down there, but had no idea the sheer volume of people who'd turned.

A hulking shape rises past the end of the bridge over what used to be downtown, but it might be my imagination: a monster mirage looming in the darkness and taking the shape of the drawings of Haven on the recruitment brochure.

Construction workers, as many as could be found, were among the first hired to work for Haven Inc., and out of steel and glass from the top floors of the downtown office and condo buildings, walls are going up above and around what was once downtown Toronto. Fed up at the inaction from City Hall, Queen's Park, and Ottawa, the presidents of the downtown banks, law firms, and other big businesses merged to seize control.

How long will we live in the dome? Months? Years? Clearly, the companies building it are banking on at least a year—but the ash clouds will clear sooner, I'm sure. Still, better safe than sorry, better in than out. Better not to think about it.

Thoughts of the future shudder through me like an earthquake so violent I need to look at everyone else to make sure the bridge isn't shaking—just me. My father's staying on the outside and assures me he'll be fine, ready to welcome us back once we leave Haven.

A body slams into the metal railing, not a metre from my face. I jump back.

Crazed eyes bulge from leathered skin, covering a man—what used to be a man—who snarls and snaps and reaches through the bars like an extra in a low-budget zombie flick. One foot's bare, big toe missing, the other wears what was once an expensive track shoe. No one jogged after the ash reached us. No one sane.

"Shredder," a voice calls and a hand grabs my shoulder, pulling me farther from the fence and the monster.

Gunfire hammers my ears and flesh flies from the creature's torso but there's little blood, as if he's composed of beef jerky. They say Shredders don't eat, don't drink—just breathe the heavy ash the rest of us try to avoid. The creature's hands, knuckles worn to the bone, don't release the railing even as police bullets mince his carcass.

Bile chokes my throat. I turn to run towards the line, my mother and brother. All my worldly belongings bounce on my back, reminding me that fewer than three months earlier, I was flirting with European backpacking plans for my last pre-university summer. Pressured by my best friend Shauna, I weighed fun and cultural experiences against my planned research internship.

Now Europe's gone. Probably. What isn't a crater is presumably buried in lava and ash.

The last contact off this continent was soon after the first asteroids struck, before we stopped getting news, before the volcanoes and earthquakes and fires, before the ash clouds clogged the air and blocked the sun, before people started dying—and worse.

My throat pinches. My best friend Shauna's gone, too. Her whole family's dead. They did it together after not being hired. Better than changing, I suppose, but I won't die on purpose. I won't take off my mask.

A roar bursts from the far end of the bridge and I spin towards the gate.

Dad. My stinging eyes blink tears onto my cheeks. Somewhere back there my father's alone, couldn't even get an application because of his asthma. Seems to me people with breathing difficulties should get top priority, but even Dad argued that the people hired to work in the dome should be those with the best chance to survive, to rebuild the world.

A section of gate falls and the crash reverberates in discordant harmony to the wails from the valley, then gunfire erupts as the crazed crowd spills through the gap, its members shot down like video game villains.

"Jenna!" Mom, holding my baby brother Felix on one hip, reaches back for me. "We've got to keep moving."

The line's rushing towards Haven's entrance now, so we run too, fighting to keep our place in the line. Mom stumbles to one knee and I pull Felix from her arms—I should have offered sooner—and his eyes are wide, full of terror, but he doesn't make a sound as he clings to my neck, clamping his little legs around my ribs, instinctively making himself easier to carry.

While Mom's down, at least six people pass us, taking our place in line. "Go," Mom yells from the gritty asphalt, but I shake my head and offer my hand. She rises and limps beside us. Forced to abandon Dad, the three of us must stick together. Our fractured family.

Fewer than ten people remain between Haven's entrance and us when the heavy doors start to shut. No way will they keep letting the line through once that mob gets close. The entrance guard checks a tall man's papers then gestures for him to pass. A woman wearing a military-style gas mask shoves me aside and Felix slips down my hip. I bounce him higher.

We won't make it. We'll be too late. Who knows if they'll ever open the east gate again and we'll never make it to the north one. The army bombed the Bayview bridge and we'd never get across the Shredder-filled Don Valley.

Gripping my brother, I race forward, pushing everyone I encounter, then thrusting our envelope towards the guard, I reach past a woman holding the hands of two kids about six and eight, both crying. It's no time to be kind. No time to care about common courtesy or fairness or rules.

When the guard takes our envelope, I turn back and yell, "Mom! Hurry."

But she stands, nailed to the bridge at least forty metres back where I left her, as if she's forgotten how to move. Behind my frozen mother, the throng nears the bridge's midpoint where the police and their guns have formed a black line, thinning the mob's progress.

"Mom!" My voice erupts in a screech almost as hideous as the noises rising up from the valley, but she shakes her head. Panic sparks my neck and a vise clamps my temples, squeezing. What is she doing? Why doesn't she come?

The guard snaps the paper drawn from our envelope, then reads, "Beth Solis, age 39." He glances at me and shrugs. "Felix Solis, age 28 months." He gestures us through the gate. "Childcare worker. Sector Four."

I jab at the contract. "And Jenna, age 17, medical training." He forgot to list me. Plus he got Mom's job wrong. She's a theoretical physicist and I made my career plans clear in my interview.

He returns our paper. "Lady, you gave me an employment contract for Beth and Felix Solis."

I shake my head and scan the words, unable to focus. "There's a mistake. There should be a Jenna listed." I know I was hired. Mom and Dad told me I got a job inside Haven on the same day they broke the horrible news that we'd have to leave Dad behind. "I'm going to be a doctor."

"Says here: Childcare." The guard's voice is flat, and a man with bony fingers pushes me from behind.

"Next." The guard reaches for the envelope of the man, who clearly jumped ahead of that family too.

Forced forward, I crane my neck, trying to see through the closing door. "Mom?" She'll straighten this out.

But she's backed away, closer to the mob, closer to the police, closer to the bullets. She blows a kiss before she's swallowed by the rising tide and I stand there, blinking, confused.

Then the truth grabs my throat, seizes my esophagus, and slams it shut. I can't believe what I'm thinking. It can't be. She wouldn't. I want to rush out after her, drag her back. It was supposed to be her who was saved. Not me. They didn't want me. I'm supposed to be out in the ash. I'm supposed to be fighting for my life with Dad. My mind clouds and thickens.

Felix whimpers, leans his sweaty curls against the bare skin at the base of my throat and, realizing I'm digging my fingers into his little leg, I loosen my grip and press a hard kiss onto his hot forehead. "It's okay, Felix Bobelix. I've got you."

Vision blurred, I let others guide me until I stand in front of a desk where a woman dressed in a navy business suit takes my contract, stamps it, hands it back.

"Beth and Felix. Welcome," she says. "You're Haven employee numbers 1-4-63-254 and 255. Please report to Sector Four."

"But ..." My voice won't work, won't tell her I'm not Beth, that I'm Jenna.

She squeezes my arm. "You can take your masks off, Beth. You and your son are safe."

What Inspired Me to Write This Selection

"The spark for this story came when global travel was interrupted by the 2010 eruption of the volcano Eyjafjallajökull in Iceland. I imagined what might happen if the world suffered a similar event but on a much larger and more catastrophic scale. Would governments react quickly enough? If they couldn't save everyone, how would they choose? And what if corporations stepped in instead? All these ideas sparked my upcoming novels in The Dust Chronicles. "Out of the Ashes" is set about seventy-five years before the novels. While it's only loosely tied to the novels, in my imagination, the little boy is the grandfather of Glory, my heroine in Deviants."

After

1. **Understanding Form and Style** Look online or in the library to find a description of the science fiction genre. What aspects of this story make it clear that it is science fiction?

2. **Reading for Meaning** What decision did Jenna's mother and father make without Jenna's knowledge? Why do you think they made this decision?

3. **Understanding Form and Style**
   a) Record at least two examples of similes in this story.
   b) What effect do these similes have on the mood of the story?

4. **Student Voice** Haven has space for only a small percentage of the population.
   a) List and explain the criteria you would use to determine who should be let into Haven.
   b) Hold a class discussion to try to reach a consensus on the five most important criteria.

5. **Speaking and Listening** Role-play a scenario in which the mother and Jenna are arguing outside the gate about which one of them should live in Haven. Respond to your partner's arguments using clear reasoning and appropriate tone and dialogue. A third student will play the guard who listens to both sides and then makes the final decision about who goes through the gate.

6. **Critical Literacy** Who has the author given power to in this story? What groups of people seem to be powerless?

7. **Metacognition** As you read, you asked questions about the situation and the setting. How did asking these questions help you understand the story?

Beyond

Student Voice The author explains that this story is a prologue to novels that are set seventy-five years later. Fill in the gap and imagine what happens to Jenna and Felix after they arrive in Haven. Continue their story in the form of a chapter of a novel or a short graphic novel, or by acting out a scene.

ON THIN ICE

Short Story

Written by John Lemon

I was raised on our family farm north of Maryfield, Saskatchewan, along with my twin sister and two older sisters. I played a variety of sports as a kid, but most of my time was spent helping my dad around our farm, such as driving and fixing machinery, fencing, and working with cattle. My future aspiration is to assume responsibility for the entire family farm.

Before

Think about the title of this short story. What different meanings are possible for the phrase "on thin ice"?

During

As you read, think about the descriptive language the author uses to create imagery in this story. Try to visualize the landscape and the actions of the characters.

Tips

imagery: use of sensory details to evoke a mental picture

climax: the most intense point in a plot, which involves a turning point in action

Frankie was startled from his sleep when his dad called upstairs, "Time to wake up!" The day had finally come; his long-awaited seventeenth birthday. Then his dad shouted, "I need help with some chores!" Frankie wondered why his father was making him work on his birthday, his one special day of the year.

When Frankie trudged outside, he was surprised to see a brand-new quad in his driveway. It was a gorgeous yellow and black 800 Can-Am ATV with shining handlebars. He couldn't wait to jump on his new wheels and take the quad for a spin. He immediately ran into the house and called his friends Joey and Allen, who also had quads. He knew they would be just as excited as he was. They arranged to meet at his house in an hour, and those sixty minutes dragged by like they were never going to end.

After Joey and Allen arrived, the boys raced down to the ravine where they knew they'd find lots of dangerous jumps and hills. Since it was March, there were snowbanks and mud holes to plow through, and ice to slide around on. They inspected each other's quads to see whose machine had the most power to attack the highest snowbanks and deepest holes.

Frankie and his two friends raced to find out whose quad was the fastest. The mud-splattered Can-Am won the race easily. The other quads were no match for Frankie's brand-new beast. Joey came in second, and Allen raced in shortly behind him.

"Ha!" Frankie laughed. "From now on, you guys are never gonna beat me!"

"Oh yeah?" said Joey as he revved his engine.

Next, they tested their quads in the huge snowdrifts that covered every hill. Laughing and joking, all of them ended up getting stuck a bunch of times. Luckily, Joey had a winch on his quad, which helped to pull them out.

The adventure seekers then tried to conquer some sticky mud. In no time at all, they were covered in it. The boys climbed towering hills, racing to see who could make it to the top. Frankie's Can-Am won every competition. The other quads didn't stand a chance. Joey had only a beat-up Honda 450 and Allen had a second-hand Polaris 500.

After the fuel gauges dropped, the boys grew tired of all the contests. They decided to look for something else to do. Scanning the low valley hills, they looked for the next challenge.

"There!" Allen spotted a glaring sheet of ice, deep in rugged ravine. Their imaginations went wild with the endless fun they could have on the sparkling ice.

"You sure it's solid?" asked Joey.

"Are you chicken or something? Afraid I'm going to beat you again?" Frankie gunned his quad.

They flew down to the open ice, racing from one end to the other, sliding wildly on the slippery surface. The three of them ripped circle after circle, daring each other to push their quads even faster. Allen and Joey lost control and crashed into each other, but smiles still shone on their faces. They were having a great time.

Crack! In an instant, the glistening ice crumbled. The boys' playfulness was pulled out from under them like a rug. The three boys and their quads dropped out of sight, deep into the ice-cold water. There was a strange silence. The broken ice bobbed on the freezing water where the boys had fallen through.

Frankie burst to the surface first, frozen and disoriented. His limbs seized up and his wet clothes pulled him back under into the dark abyss. When he resurfaced, he frantically searched for his two friends. He yelled and screamed, praying for them to come up from the frigid water. Frankie didn't know how much longer he could stay afloat. Finally, Joey and Allen appeared, terrified and gasping for air. The boys desperately swam to the edge of the ice. They had to get out, and quick.

The boys struggled to escape the grasp of the ice-cold water. The ice constantly broke beneath them and they kept falling through. Minutes passed, but it felt like hours. Finally the boys pulled themselves free of the icy tentacles. The solid, dry land was like heaven.

Thankful to be alive, they looked back to see the gaping hole that had consumed their three quads. What would their dads say? Would they be angry or would they be thankful that they still had their sons? They all agreed that their dads' anger would probably kill each of them. Frankie's dad would be especially crazy, because the brand new quad was now lying at the bottom of the frozen ravine.

"C'mon guys. We'd better get going before it gets too dark." Frankie was already feeling the cold stiffening his limbs. They'd have to worry about all the fury when they arrived home, if they ever made it home. They had roughly two and a half miles to walk, through bush and hills. They were soaking wet with frozen clothes and shivering bodies.

The frigid wind ripped at their skin, but they kept on walking. Their bodies were numb to the bone, but they kept walking. The hope of a warm home and dry clothes kept their determination and spirits alive. The sun slowly set.

"H-hh-oww much f-f-further?" Joey stammered.

Frankie could barely feel his lips, "Not ... far ... now."

Back home, each family grew tense with worry. Frankie's dad hopped in his red truck and sped down to the ravine to look for the boys. They saw the headlights coming down the hill towards them. They were filled with joy and relief.

Frankie's dad rushed them into the heated truck and then drove straight to the hospital. The boys had extreme frostbite and slight cases of hypothermia. They were kept overnight for observation.

The next day Frankie, Joey, and Allen had regained most of their strength. They explained the story to their families. No one was as angry as the boys thought they would be. Frankie's parents never left his bedside. When they left the hospital, Frankie breathed a sigh of relief, "Man, we were lucky."

Frankie's dad answered gruffly, "Yeah, now you can start working off the cost of that quad."

Frankie stuttered, "But, I ... I ... I thought you said that you were happy that we're alive!"

"Of course I am. But who's going to pay for that quad?"

What Inspired Me to Write This Selection

" My favourite pastimes include playing hockey, hunting, and driving around on my snowmobile and quad. Many times when my friends and I went out on our quads, we wouldn't think of the consequences of our actions. Although we were lucky and avoided serious injury, some of our fun-loving and innocent exploits could have resulted in tragedy. I wrote this story to reveal how quickly a simple adventure can turn into disaster. "

After

1. **Reading for Meaning** Why do you think the boys went out on the ice with their quads? Support your answer with evidence from the story.

2. **Reading for Meaning** What was Frankie's dad's reaction to his accident? Choose the best answer below.
   A. He was just happy that Frankie was alive and didn't care that his new quad was ruined.
   B. He was angry that Frankie had wrecked his new quad.
   C. He was happy that Frankie was alive, but wanted him to know there are consequences for his actions.
   D. He was proud that Frankie knew what to do in an emergency.

3. **Understanding Form and Style**
   a) What is the climax of this story?
   b) Could you see the climax coming? Explain why or why not.

4. **Viewing and Representing**
   a) What moment(s) in the story would you choose to depict if you were the person to decide what art would appear with this story? Why?
   b) Visually depict the moment(s) you identified in part (a) using hand-drawn or computer-generated illustrations or photographs.

5. **Student Voice** In your opinion, is it fair for Frankie's father to make him pay for the quad, which he gave him as a gift?

6. **Student Voice** Was the fact that the boys survived their accident believable? Explain why or why not.

7. **Critical Literacy** Do you think the author intended the reader to feel sympathy for the boys in this story? Why or why not?

8. **Metacognition**
   a) Did trying to visualize what was going on in this story help you to understand it? Why or why not?
   b) How did visualizing affect your engagement with and enjoyment of the story?

Beyond

Creating Media Texts Choose an extreme sport. Create a poster, brochure, or short video that either promotes the sport or warns of the dangers involved in the sport. Teens are your target audience, so use techniques and content that would appeal to them.

MOVING MOUNTAINS

Short Story

Written by Shawn Elgby

I was born in Qalandarabad, Pakistan, to missionary parents. I spent the earlier years of my life moving around from Pakistan to Caronport, Saskatchewan, to Calgary, Alberta, and finally Maryfield, Saskatchewan. When I graduated high school, I decided to attend Bible college. I first started writing small picture books before kindergarten (mostly about dinosaurs). Today I still love to write, and I seek to honour God through my writing and my life in general.

Tips

inference: meaning reached by a reader based on what the author states or implies as well as the reader's prior knowledge or experience

dialogue: conversation between two or more people in a story

first-person point of view: the perspective of a character in the story as he or she experiences it. It can be identified by the use of the pronoun *I* throughout.

third-person point of view: the perspective of the narrator, who is not a character in the story

epilogue: a concluding section added to a literary work, such as a story, novel, or play

Before

What does courage mean to you? Give an example of a courageous act that you have seen or heard of. Explain why you think it is courageous.

During

1. As you read, visualize what the author is describing. Pay attention to how the images in your head change as you read more.
2. As you read, make predictions about how you think the story will end.

Flames lick the falling piece of charred oak as it crashes on the soot-stained rug. My eyes burst open as shards of blackened wood rain down from the ceiling. I spring up and bolt into the next room. A small body buried under a warm Spiderman comforter sleeps peacefully, oblivious to the growing blaze. I grab my little brother and dash into the living room. Boards crash and glass shatters as the intense heat of the flowing red mist smothers the apartment.

I'm still groggy but I'm trying to make sense of what is happening. Where are my mom and dad? I have to save them too! And then, it all comes back to me.

"Bye, Mom," said little Ben, "have a good time."

"We will," replied my mom as she turned to me. "Quinn, be sure he has enough blankets on his bed. It's going to be cold these next few nights. Oh, and make sure he eats all of his vegetables, and …"

"Don't worry, Ellen," interrupted my father. "They are going to be fine."

"Yeah. Don't worry, Mom," I said, exchanging a hug with her and a handshake with my father. "I'll take good care of Ben."

I snap out of my reverie and set Ben down in a safe corner of the room. Our small apartment is flooded with smoke but I can see that the flames have already engulfed the hallway to our front door. I rattle and shake the living room window that Dad has always meant to fix, but it's stuck. The flames are scaling the side of the building like Ben's favourite superhero.

Spotting another possible escape route, I pull a chair over to the wall and reach up to grab the steel grate of an air vent. As the metal burns into my soft flesh, I cry out and pull away my shaking hand.

A flurry of ideas storm my desperate mind. I snatch up a metal broom from the kitchen and force the handle into the grate. The sound of grinding metal scrapes and claws at my ears. I force the broom into the grate. "Leverage," I whisper to myself. "What I need is leverage." Mustering all my strength, I tug at the unforgiving, useless lever. "C'mon," I groan as the broom begins to bend. "Please come out." The broom continues to bend, but the grate mocks my efforts. I can't understand it. When I was a kid and I got into trouble, I used to be able to pull the grate out and hide from my parents in the air vent. But the cruel heat of the fire has made it swell, blocking our escape.

As I turn to go to the kitchen in search of another tool to remove the grate, I see a small piece of Ben's comforter starting to smoke. I run to him and rip the comforter from his white-knuckled hands. He lets out a blood-curdling scream. His only security in the face of a supreme foe is gone. The soft cotton of the bedspread bursts into a calm and flowing fire like a soft candle. I hold the sobbing boy as tight as I can.

He lays his head on my shoulder and wraps his sweaty arms around my neck. I run my hands through his damp hair, kiss his tender head, and calm him. He snuggles into my arms and I know he trusts me. My throbbing mind is weak and cannot think of anything that can save us now.

But … I think I hear voices. Yes, I do hear voices; they are calling out from the other side of the lake of fire. I scream back, "We're in here! HELP!"

My heart nearly leaps from my chest as I hear firefighters shouting. Can it be? Will this nightmare end?

"We're coming in to get you. Just stay calm," yells an angelic voice from the other side of hell.

Those words fill my entire being with hope. I stand up to greet our saviours when I hear a huge explosion, and the floor beneath me shivers and quakes. The heat in our small apartment quickly becomes unbearable. Though it's barely audible, I can hear a voice, "I'm sorry. I'm so sorry. We have to turn back."

"NO, NO!" I scream, "YOU CAN'T LEAVE! YOU CAN'T!"

I cannot stop the tears and I cannot let go of Ben. My breath is kicked out of me with every sob. I look around the room, but my eyes are so blurred with my tears, all I see is a haze.

"It's going to be okay," a soft voice whispers in my ear. "You'll think of something."

My brother believes that I can do anything, that I can move mountains for him. I hold him tighter and weep in his ear. "Sure I will, Ben," I lie, "sure I will."

I dry my tears and look around the room, a sudden, cool gust of wind seems to speak to me as it flows through my hair. It beckons me to a gaping hole in the wall, eaten away by the indifferent blaze. I stare blankly through the hole and see skyscrapers in the distance, tearing through the darkness and forming a panorama of light. My weary mind slowly accepts the last resort. There is no way out. There is no escape. I've fought and lost. It's over. I walk

towards the hole, holding Ben's tiny figure in my arms, when a barrage of boards and debris falls from the smoking roof. I quickly toss Ben to the side as the pile of rubble crushes my legs. The weight of the mound snaps my bones like twigs and pins me to the ground. Ben runs over to me through the dark cloud of dust and tugs at my hand, but I cannot budge. Exhausted from the fight, I hold Ben's hand and stop him from pulling me.

"Get up, Quinn," he yells, pulling on my arm once again. "It's getting closer."

I pull him to me and hold him in my arms. "It's okay, Ben," I whisper.

"No, no, you gotta get up. You gotta get up and find a way," he sobs.

I hold him tight as he sheds his hot tears on my already tear-soaked shoulder. The gaping hole lies only a foot or two behind Ben. Rubble tumbles out of the hole and falls into the dark night. We're twelve stories up, so it will take a few moments before it hits the ground.

"Do you trust me?" I ask softly.

Ben nods while gasping between his loud cries.

"Ben, close your eyes," I sorrowfully whisper into his ear. "Close them tight and don't open them. Think of the happiest place you can imagine and, I promise, when you open your eyes, you'll be there."

"Promise?" he whimpered.

"I promise," I say, trying to smile as he shuts his piercing blue eyes.

I squeeze him one last time and then release my hug. Numbly, I place my hand on his chest and push.

What Inspired Me to Write This Selection

" I wanted to write a story about an ethical idea that intrigued me: Would you kill to save a life? As I wrote, the question changed to: Would you kill someone precious to you in order to spare them from a cruel death? This question was the driving force behind this story. In writing this story, I came to the conclusion that true love is fully shown in true sacrifice. One key person who taught me to love writing and storytelling was my English teacher, Mrs. Frazer. "

After

1. **Reading for Meaning**   Were your predictions about the story's ending correct? Explain.

2. **Reading for Meaning**   Why do you think Quinn pushed his little brother out of the building? Use evidence from the text to make your inferences.

3. **Viewing and Representing**   Make a story board or flow chart that shows the sequence of important events that happen in this story.

4. **Understanding Form and Style**   This story was written from the first-person point of view. What problem does this point of view cause for the plot? Explain how the author could have avoided this problem.

5. **Understanding Form and Style**   Think about what this story would be like without the dialogue. What role does the dialogue have in this story?

6. **Speaking and Listening**   Consider how different dialogue could change the plot of the story. Work with a partner and rewrite the dialogue from this story. Role-play this revised dialogue with your partner.

7. **Student Voice**   Imagine you were in the same situation as Quinn, the main character in this story. What would you have done differently? If you would have done the same things, explain why.

8. **Critical Literacy**   Although this story is about a fire, it is also about the relationship between two brothers. Explain the values and beliefs the author communicates through this relationship.

9. **Metacognition**   How did visualizing what you were reading affect your understanding of the story?

Beyond

Reading for Meaning   Imagine what happens after this story ends. Choose one of the following activities:
- Write an epilogue to continue the story from a third-person point of view.
- Write a newspaper article that covers the events in this story. Be sure to include only parts of the story that a journalist would know about. Remember to cover the 5 W's (who, what, when, where, why) when writing the article.

HOLDING HARLEY

Short Story

Written by Jocelyn Shipley

Jocelyn Shipley's books for teens include *Getting a Life* and *Seraphina's Circle*, and she is also co-editor of *Cleavage: Breakaway Fiction*. Her latest YA novel, *How to Tend a Grave*, was published in 2012. Jocelyn has lived in Canberra, Australia, although she now lives on Vancouver Island and in Toronto.

Before

Harley, in the title of this story, is a baby born to a teenaged mom. Who do you predict will be the narrator of this first-person narrative? Give reasons for your answer.

During

As you read, try to make connections to the events of this story and to the emotions felt by the narrator. If you can't connect personally, think of connections you can make between this story and other fictional or real-life stories that you know of.

I want everybody to know that I'm sorry and I'd do anything, anything at all, to hold Harley again. And, okay, I have to admit that Mom was right. Shaela should never have had a kid at seventeen, with no job, no partner, and just me, her younger brother, to help her. But my sister was so sure she could raise him herself and finish high school too. "There's always money somewhere," she said, "if you know where to look and how to work the system."

When Mom heard Shaela barfing on a Sunday morning, she yelled at her for drinking too much. But Shaela yelled back, "Guess what? I'm not hung over—I'm pregnant! You're gonna be a Granny!"

"Not on your life."

That's pretty much how Shaela's boyfriend felt about things too. So Shaela left and I went with her since I was ready to go anyway. At first it was fun, like a big exciting adventure.

We thought we could manage. One of Shaela's friends had a baby on her own and things had worked out not so bad. But that friend's parents supported her decision. They loved that baby and were the best grandparents ever. Mom wasn't taking Shaela out shopping for cute little baby clothes or organizing a shower or letting Shaela live at home with her kid.

Shaela rented a crappy basement apartment for us with money she had from our dad, money she was supposed to be saving for college. I worked at a pizza place besides going to school. Shaela quit smoking and drinking. She found a doctor and made a birth plan and went to counselling and all.

I went to prenatal classes with her so I could be her birthing coach. Everybody else was way older and they looked at us weird, especially the pregnant women. I don't think they liked Shaela's ink, and for sure they didn't like how she flirted with the dads and showed off her bump. Nobody talked to us, but they were always dissing teen parents loud enough for us to hear.

Anyway, after Shaela went through about three days of labour, begging for drugs and threatening to kill me, her ex-boyfriend, and every other male on the planet, Harley finally popped out. He was kind of blue and all covered with blood and this cheesy slime and he was screaming like the doctor was murdering him, but he was the most beautiful, the most amazing thing I've ever seen.

I've never felt that way about anybody before. Not even a girl. After Shaela held him, I had a turn, and I thought I'd die of joy. I finally had a purpose in life. I was going to be the best uncle ever.

For his first six months, Harley was with me whenever I wasn't at school or work. He'd make these sweet baby sounds that I'm sure were him trying to talk to me and he'd smile and wave his little hands around. Shaela said he wasn't really talking, just babbling like all babies do. But I know that when he went da, da, da, he was trying to say my name, Darcy.

At school all the kids who had trash-talked Shaela started saying how great we were doing and how cool I was for helping her. When I picked Harley up from the onsite daycare, hot girls who never would have spoken to me before called me Daddy Darcy and asked to hold Harley and play with him. Apparently females of any age just can't resist a guy with a baby.

Except for Mom. I always figured that if she would just hold Harley she'd be as hooked as I am. He's a perfect baby with his chubby face and big eyes and drooly smile. But Mom won't give in. She came to the hospital once and looked at him, but she wouldn't hold him. That's right—she did not take him in her arms. She has never once held her grandson.

We were mostly doing okay though, those first months, except that Shaela was slipping back into her old ways. And then two days ago, she disappeared. She left early in the morning while Harley and I were still asleep. Probably took the bus into the city. I sure hope she's not crashing somewhere in Downtown Eastside, because for such a smart girl, she sure knows how to screw up.

I guess I should have seen it coming. I mean, I knew she was struggling, not going to classes and all, but I didn't think she'd actually leave us. Here's what she wrote on a page from her math notebook:

Sorry Darcy, but I can't cope anymore. Tell Mom it's only for a little while. I just need a break to get myself back together. Look after Harley for me, okay?

After I found Shaela's note, I skipped school, called in sick to work, and hung out with Harley. I didn't want to tell Mom that Shaela was gone. But then we ran out of formula and rice cereal and diapers. I didn't have any money and Harley was crying and then he started screaming, so I had to do something. I took him over to Mom, because I'm not his dad after all, I'm just his uncle and what else was I supposed to do?

I put Harley in his sling and walked over. It was the first time I'd been back since he was born. When I got there, Mom was sleeping, because she works nights at the nursing home. She hates being woken up, so she was really cranky when she came to the door. "What's up?" she said in her suspicious whatever-you've-done-it's-wrong voice. Then she stood there in her plush white robe—the one she stole from a hotel the time she and Dad went to Vegas—with her arms crossed over her heart like she had to actually stop herself from holding Harley.

"Shae's gone. We need help."

Mom gave me her you-disgust-me look. She didn't even glance at Harley. Then she pulled her robe tighter and let me in.

I sat at the kitchen table with Harley asleep in his sling. The fabric was midnight blue, printed with tiny moons and stars, and he looked angelic, even though he smelled rank. I wrapped my arms around him and told Mom about Shaela leaving and not calling and then I bawled like Harley had been doing earlier.

I so missed being at home and being looked after, even if Mom was always critical of everything I did.

"Right," Mom said and grabbed the phone.

"Please don't make that call," I begged. "It's just for a little while, and then Shae will come back." I knew that was probably not going to happen, but I had to try. Then I said, "If you won't help us for Shaela, then do it for Harley. Think of Harley."

Mom gave me a sick little smile and said, "Exactly." Then she started punching in the number. She didn't even have to look up it up. She must have had it memorized, because she'd been so sure that this would happen.

"Mom, please!"

"Sorry. I warned you both."

I couldn't believe she'd really call social services on us, and I guess Shaela never thought she would either. But Mom had threatened she would from the start. "After you have this baby," she'd told Shaela, "don't think I'm your backup. Don't think I'll take you in if you can't manage. I'm not your granny-nanny and I'm not raising another kid after you two."

The social worker came that afternoon and she even had a cop with her just in case. But I was so tired and scared I didn't resist. I'm ashamed to say this now, but I let them take Harley without a fight. Sure, we'd gotten through so far, but it was so hard with never enough money/food/sleep. Plus a few times I was worried that Shaela was going to lose it and get violent. She'd punched me a few times and I didn't want her hurting Harley.

But Shaela walking out was hurting him too. I was pretty mad at her for that. So at the time I figured maybe Harley would be better off in foster care, or maybe even adopted if Shaela would ever sign the papers.

But then after they took Harley, I freaked out and trashed Mom's house. I couldn't stop myself. At least Mom didn't press charges, but I'll have to pay for everything I wrecked. Like her collection of china dolls. How could she possibly love those stupid ugly things more than Harley?

And now I can't stop wondering where Harley is and who's looking after him and are they holding him? I want him back so bad that if I knew where he was, I'd go kidnap him. I'd run away with him and we'd live in the rainforest or on an island somewhere. No one would ever find us.

I know you said that eventually I can have supervised visits, but won't that just make things worse? How can I look into Harley's face and have him all smiley and happy to see me and then tell him I won't be in his life like I was?

Oh man, I can't deal with this. *Look after Harley for me, okay?* Shaela's note said. But I didn't. I lost him and Mom said it will be really hard to get him back. Practically impossible. And that's if Shaela ever even shows up again.

"You don't have to feel guilty," Mom said. "You did the right thing and she can't blame you."

Wow, that's so comforting.

You said it will help if I can talk about it. Or write things down if that would be easier. But there's this Harley-size hole in my heart. And there's nothing I can possibly say or write that will ever fix that.

I just have to trust that Harley knows how much I love him. I hope he knows how much I want to be with him and how totally helpless I feel. And, more than anything, I hope somebody's holding him right now.

What Inspired Me to Write This Selection

❝ When I was in high school, teen pregnancy was shocking and scandalous. Girls were hidden away in homes for unwed mothers and usually gave their babies up for adoption. But now there is support and acceptance, which seems much more humane. Even so, it can be very difficult for teens to be responsible parents. I began writing 'Holding Harley' to explore such a situation from a teen mom's point of view, but then her brother Darcy fell for Harley and took over the story. ❞

After

1. **Reading for Meaning**   Who do you think Darcy is addressing at the beginning and ending of the text? Why is he addressing this person(s)? What is he trying to accomplish?

2. **Understanding Form and Style**   Analyze the author's diction and her use of imagery and dialogue. How successful was she at making Darcy's actions and emotions authentically male? Use examples from the story to support your answer.

3. **Student Voice**   Before Harley was born, the mother warned Shaela she would not help her raise the baby. The mother stuck to her word and refused even to look at her grandson when Darcy brought Harley to her house. In your opinion, is it a parent's responsibility to help his or her teenage child care for a baby? Explain why or why not.

4. **Viewing and Representing**   Analyze the illustrations that accompany this story. Do you think they do a good job of depicting the emotions in this story? Explain your thinking.

5. **Critical Literacy**   Consider the author's inspiration note as well as her portrayal of Shaela in this story. If this author were giving a high school lecture on teen pregnancy, what might she say? What advice might she give?

6. **Metacognition**   Explain how any prior knowledge you had about teen pregnancy affected your understanding of the actions and emotions of the characters in this story.

Beyond

Creating Media Texts   Do some research to find out what support is available to teen parents living in your province or territory. Choose one of these services or programs and design a newspaper, online, or radio advertisement that would appeal to young people such as Darcy and Shaela.

I Am From...

Poetry

Written by Zack Praill, Isobel Scott, George Ladouceur, Brogan Ho, and Richard Chang

Tips

imagery: the use of sensory details to evoke a mental picture. Imagery appeals to any of the five senses: sight, sound, taste, touch, or smell.

symbolic: representing something using symbols; for example, a flag is symbolic of a country

Before

This is a collection of poems students have written about themselves. What information or insights might you gain from reading these poems?

During

As you read, write one question or comment you have about each poem.

By Zack Praill

I am an 18-year-old high school student from Chatham, Ontario. I have always enjoyed English because writing came easier to me than other subjects. This poem is about where I am from and the positive and negative experiences in my life, which have shaped me thus far.

I am from a one-level, red-brick ranch-style house with white siding and a yard ambushed by monumental pine trees.

I am from warm, spicy family suppers, and deep-dish cheesy chimichangas.

I am from hard-working parents who are always there for advice; good advice isn't always going to be taken but that doesn't mean they stop giving it when they feel it is needed.

I am from cold, icy, intense winters at Ellicottville Ski Resort vacationing with family while shredding the soft falling powder-like snow under the edges of my size-138 sexy Burton Board.

I am from quiet nights watching my favourite movies, laughing at Stiffler in *American Pie* and reminiscing with friends about how long the school week was and how great the weekend is.

I am from a successful family filled with many memorable moments from hockey championships and my mom just done fighting, and winning, her battle with cancer.

I am from a car that is pretty much driven and dependent on the loud bumps of my speakers.

I am Zack Praill, and I couldn't be happier.

By Isobel Scott

Isobel Scott is a high school student living in North Vancouver, British Columbia. She comes from a family of nurses and accountants who are really quite creative. She grew up on her Grandpa's stories, a life of good old Christian teaching, and the great outdoors. Isobel is currently working towards becoming an archaeologist and an author.

I am from jellybeans and plastic cups;
From snowboarding and ringette.
I am from England and Sweden;
And from watching movies with my dad.

I am from kershplunk in the pool on a hot day,
And from gazing longingly at museum exhibits.
I am from riding on a horse's back and going
Thump-de-thump-de-thump.

I am from many notebooks I used up with sketches,
And from all the wonderful books I have read in my life.
I am from Earth.

By George Ladouceur

I am fourteen years old and in Grade Eight at Rocky Lane School, Fort Vermilion, Alberta. I am a First Nation member from the Little Red River Cree Nation band. My poem is based on my life while living among the Inuit in Cambridge Bay, Nunavut, from Grade One to Grade Six.

I am from where the cold winds blow, hitting fifty below
I am from where the tundra unfolds the soft moss and purple flowers
I am from where the polar bears roam freely looking for something to eat
I am from where hunters hunt for caribou and seals, hunting for their families
so they can eat happily.
I am from the place where there is snow for nine months of the year
I am from the land of thousands of mosquitoes defying three cans of mosquito
spray

I am from the home of big icebergs where hunters go out in a group to go ice fishing and jump from piece to piece to avoid getting wet from big oceans of cold deep waters.

By Brogan Ho

I am fifteen years old and live in Burnaby, British Columbia. I got my start in writing when I joined the Young Writer's Club in North Vancouver five years ago. My other interests include acting, singing, piano, and traditional Chinese dance. I love being in a multicultural environment and enjoy learning foreign languages.

I am from pink and light green
I am from eating sushi every week
I am from not fitting in all the time
From mock auditions and the sides I perform at them.

I am from European and Chinese ancestors, and
From the Hapa pride shared with others of mixed descent.

I am from pixie haircuts and glasses;
From playing Dance Dance Revolution with friends, and
From watching *American Idol*.
I am from swordfighting and homeschooling.
I am from Canada.

By Richard Chang

I grew up in Etobicoke, Ontario, and have been writing poetry since middle school as a means to express myself. I love to travel and have lived in China and South Korea, teaching English to Chinese and Korean students. This poem draws on my Korean-Canadian upbringing and how my surroundings and experiences have shaped me into the person I am today.

I am from *Archie* comic books:
identified with Jughead, but wanted that Reggie Mantle look
I am from the smell of drywall
after my dad punched a hole in the wall
From a garden where fruit is grown on trees:
apples and bananas, but I am a blueberry
I am from a place where affection never entered time
Confucianism was never a friend of mine
I am from a girl turning Confucianism on its head
Yup, I said it, Confucianism is now dead
I am from a Polish deli open late, just one more pierogi
I am from somewhere lies were okay,
as long as they were used to make me obey
I am from hope, who has a name:
Grace, who likes to sing in the rain
I am from the meeting of male and female,
conceived in the land of the Holy Grail
I am from egg rice smothered in butter,
culinary skills of my grandmother
I am from laughter coming out of a bottle
Feelings finally expressed that I had once bottled
I am from a foreign land,
touched by the presence of a beautiful hand.

After

1. **Reading for Meaning** Choose one of the poems. Using details from the poem, write a descriptive paragraph about the poet.

2. **Understanding Form and Style** These poems involve a lot of imagery. Reread the poems and identify a different image for each of the five senses. Create a chart like the one below to record your answers. The images can be from any of the poems.

Sense	Image
sight	
sound	
taste	
touch	
smell	

3. **Speaking and Listening** Do a dramatic reading of one of these poems for a partner. Try to use vocal strategies—your voice, pauses, volume—to bring the poem to life. Listen carefully to your partner's reading and give feedback.

4. **Viewing and Representing** Choose one of the poems. Create a symbolic representation to accompany the poem. You may use an illustration, a painting, or collage to symbolize the ideas in the poem.

5. **Student Voice** Which poem can you most relate to? Why?

6. **Critical Literacy** Choose one of the poems. What do you know about the author's background that might help you explain the observations or statements he or she makes in the poem? Look for clues within the poem and in the author's short biography.

7. **Metacognition** How did asking questions as you read help you understand the poems?

Beyond

Student Voice Write your own "I Am From" poem, using these poems as models. Include information such as ordinary items you identify with, food you love, family traditions, family tendencies, family stories, things you were told as a child, etc.

Forms of Nonfiction

BIG IDEA ❯ **How do good writers organize information to communicate effectively?**

What are forms of nonfiction?

Nonfiction writing is based on fact. This factual information can include statistics, opinions, and autobiographical information, and can take the form of essays, magazine articles, interviews, profiles, and lists, for example. In this section, you will find nonfiction forms such as persuasive essays about the vices and virtues of professional fighting, top ten lists, and interviews with a musician and athletes.

How do I read various forms of nonfiction?

❯ **Recognize the genre**—Recognizing the genre of nonfiction text (such as an interview, an essay, or a profile) can help you know what to expect and put what you are about to read in context. For example, an interview is often presented in a question-and-answer format, while a persuasive essay usually includes statistics, examples, and expert opinion to support the author's point of view.

❯ **Pay attention to text features**—Good writers take time to structure their writing so readers can easily understand and find information. They use text features such as headings, subheadings, photo captions, and text formatting, such as bolded questions in an interview, to organize and clearly present ideas.

UFC: Robinson versus Walker

Debate

Written by Laura Robinson and Ian Walker

Before

These essays are both about mixed martial arts (MMA) and the Ultimate Fighting Championship (UFC). What do you already know about MMA and the UFC? How do you think your knowledge will affect your understanding of these two essays?

During

You may come across several unfamiliar words in these essays. As you read, use sticky notes to identify these words and develop strategies for understanding their meaning; for example, use context clues or look up the words online or in a dictionary.

Fight Night

Written by Laura Robinson

Laura Robinson is a former member of the national cycling team and a former Canadian rowing champion. When she retired from competition she became a sports journalist and author. Her books include *Crossing the Line: Violence and Sexual Assault in Canada's National Sport*; *Black Tights: Women, Sport and Sexuality*; *Great Girls: Profiles of Awesome Canadian Athletes*; and *Cyclist BikeList*. Laura still loves to ride her bike, cross-country ski, and row. Her partner, John, is her favourite partner in sports.

What if every time you went to see your favourite sport, you put your brain at risk? What if friendships with others suffer because of the changes to your brain made by watching this sport?

From 2001 to 2009, the Ultimate Fighting Championship (UFC) went from a reported $2 million outfit to over $1.5 billion (USD). This mixed martial arts (MMA) organization hosts twenty to thirty events a year, with about ten fights at each event. MMA is known as a violent no-holds-barred sport, which involves boxing, wrestling, kickboxing, *muay Thai*, karate, tae kwon do, judo, and other forms of martial arts. Young males aged eighteen to thirty-four sell out these events, with over 10 000 spectators at a single event, while thousands more watch matches on closed-circuit televisions. The United States alone has 1.3 million UFC pay-per-view subscriptions. Out of thirty sports listed in a recent Ipso-Reid poll, UFC is the fastest-growing "sport" in terms of popularity. That's a lot of people paying to harm their brain if the scientific studies on violence and its effects on the brain are correct.

In 2007, neuroscientists Christopher Kelly, Jack Grinband, and Joy Hirsch at Columbia University Medical Centre in New York experimented by looking at the part of the brain believed to control reactive aggression. This is the behaviour someone exhibits through an immediate negative reaction, inappropriate for the circumstances causing the behaviour. To measure reactions, neuroscientists used functional magnetic resonance imaging (fMRI), which lets them observe certain parts of volunteers' brains crucial to perceiving a threat. This part of the brain decides whether we act assertively or aggressively in response to other people's behaviour.

For example, say you're cycling through an intersection and a driver turns right and cuts you off. You see him parking close by and remark politely but firmly that cyclists have the same right to the road as car drivers. Your reaction is assertive. An aggressive reaction would occur if the driver responded with obscenities, telling you next time he won't miss.

What causes the driver to react with anger and aggression, instead of thinking about the danger to the cyclist and apologizing? Neuro and social scientists have long suspected exposure to violence harms thought processes. However, only recently have advances been made to allow them to watch which parts of the brain are affected when subjects view violence.

A brain scan using fMRI technology.

In 2007, the Columbia neuroscientists looked at the brain's ability to choose the most appropriate reaction to violence that is witnessed, including violent media. They showed violent video clips to fourteen volunteers and then compared responses in the brain with the volunteers' responses to nonviolent clips. The volunteers also filled out a questionnaire designed to measure aggression levels. The study showed that watching violent video clips led to a suppression in the brain's ability to inhibit (or stop) inappropriate aggressive behaviour. The results of the questionnaire supported these findings.

Social scientists are equally interested in human response to violence. In 2009, at the University of Michigan's Institute for Social Research, professors Brad Bushman and Craig Anderson were interested in the impact playing violent video games has on us if, at the same time, others needed our help. Volunteers watched twenty minutes of violent videos while other volunteers watched nonviolent videos. A fight was staged in the hallway outside the lab where participants filled out a questionnaire about the videos. Volunteers who watched the nonviolent videos stopped writing sooner, leaving to help the "injured victim" faster than those watching the violent videos, who took more than 4½ times longer before helping.

The experiment leader started to fill out a campus-police report, and asked volunteers to describe the fight. The violent video volunteers believed the fight was not nearly as violent as the nonviolent video volunteers thought it was.

The researchers staged a second experiment outside a movie theatre that screened a violent film and a nonviolent film. As patrons waited, a young woman with an injured ankle struggled to pick up her crutches. Patrons waiting for both films came to her aid at the same time. But when she struggled with the crutches as they filed out of the movie theatre, nonviolent film patrons helped sooner. The authors of the study titled it, "Comfortably Numb: Desensitizing Effects of Violent Media on Helping Others."

It's unfair, though, to target just UFC. Two thousand other studies conducted over the past twenty years also show a relationship between viewing violence and aggressive behaviour. UFC is only one form of violence. How do domestic violence, school-yard and street violence, violent movies, TV shows, video games, and pro hockey affect our spirit, bodies, and brains? The Vancouver Stanley Cup riots showed disturbing behaviour, especially when we look at statistics from the Vancouver Police Department on reported sexual

Police officers hold back the crowd on a Vancouver street after rioters burned police cars in the wake of the Vancouver Canucks loss to the Boston Bruins in the NHL's Stanley Cup Final in 2011.

offences. District 1 of Vancouver, the entertainment district with the highest percentage of sports bars, saw unprecedented levels of sexual assaults reported during the play-offs in April and May 2011. How is on-ice hockey violence related to off-ice violence?

One year before the Stanley Cup riots, Dr. Graham Pollett, medical officer for health with the Middlesex-London Health Unit, wrote the report "Keep Mixed Martial Arts Illegal in Ontario." He argues that MMA should be illegal in Ontario, noting that the Middlesex-London Board of Health had "taken a stand against violence in hockey as part of an approach to utilize sports as a means of educating boys and men in how to address highly emotional, conflict situations without resorting to violence as part of achieving the overall objective of addressing violence in society, particularly violence against women and children."

Dr. Pollett believes if violence is used to make boys and young men understand how to "perform" masculinity, then "the cumulative result of repeated exposure to violence through sports, video games, movies, etc. is to desensitize people to the negative and harmful effects of violence. For children, this is exhibited in a number of ways including aggressive behaviour."

Do you want your brain to no longer stop you from reacting aggressively when the situation doesn't call for it? Do you want your exposure to violent media to stop you from caring for and helping people in need? If not, think about what you're exposing your brain to when you turn on the television. As you get older, teachers', parents', and even older siblings' voices will gradually be replaced by your own inner voice—your conscience. What will yours be saying?

What Inspires Me to Write

> " I knew I was going to be a writer in Grade Eight after my teacher gave a group of us interesting novels to read and told us to discuss them. I loved the feeling of being swept away by words, and wanted the ability to do this. At the same time, I had started to seriously ride a bike and cross-country ski competitively. Those sports also swept me away. They took me to what I call my foreign land—a place where time stretches and retracts, where anything can happen. When I am on my bike or skis, I feel the same way I do when I read a really good story—as if I am no longer on Earth. "

Let's Have a Clean Fight

Written by Ian Walker

Ian Walker is an NHL and Vancouver Canucks beat writer with the *Vancouver Sun*, where his past responsibilities have included the CFL, Vancouver Whitecaps, junior hockey, and extreme sports, as well as being a features writer at the 2010 Winter Olympics. His conversational style of writing has been featured in newspapers and magazines across Canada, and he is a regular contributor with the *National Post, UMM, Canadian Business, Real Golf*, and *TV Week*, to name just a few.

There's no denying that in the earliest days of the Ultimate Fighting Championship (UFC), it was sheer violence and mayhem. There were very few, if any, rules; no weight classes; and fighters didn't wear gloves, if you can believe it.

But wait, that's not even the worst of it. The *coup de grace* had to be when the UFC's founder, Campbell McLaren, went on American network TV and boasted to the world that there were only three ways to win a fight: tapout, knockout, or death.

So it's no wonder then, that U.S. Senator John McCain famously likened the sport to human cockfighting. Heck, looking back, he was probably right.

For, in its infancy, the UFC was truly a no-holds-barred example of the decline of civilization; a sport so barbaric, so savage, that few provinces or states even dared sanction the events.

But that was then. This is now. The UFC has evolved. So too should our view of the fight league.

That's right, no longer is mixed martial arts (MMA) an underground cult favourite of the great unwashed, but rather a mainstream sports behemoth and cultural phenomenon, worth in excess of $1.5 billion (USD). Worldwide, UFC has offices in the United States, Canada, England, and China and is accessible in a half-billion homes in 175 different countries and 20 different languages.

More impressive yet, not only is the UFC the largest MMA promoter in the world, but it is in direct competition with the big four North American sports leagues: the National Hockey League, the National Basketball Association, the National Football League, and Major League Baseball.

Not coincidentally, it's also under new ownership, but more about that later.

Today's UFC is home to some of the world's most elite athletes. MMA is arguably the most demanding sport on earth, if not one of the oldest. With roots that can be traced back to 648 BC, when it was known as *pankration*, which is Greek for "all powers," MMA allows the use of both striking and grappling techniques, both standing and on the ground, and can include, but is not limited to, boxing, wrestling, Brazilian *jiujitsu*, *muay Thai*, kickboxing, karate, and judo.

Still, despite these differences in style, all UFC fighters share a few common traits, including an incredible work ethic and a tremendous amount of self-discipline. Make no mistake about it, these are men who have dedicated their adult lives to their

Detail of an ancient Greek relief showing a *pankration* fighting match, a martial art that involved both wrestling and boxing techniques.

profession, not unlike a doctor or lawyer. While critics care to see the UFC only as something as visceral as two men beating on each other in a cage, MMA is as complex and technical as ballet.

Now before we go any further, let's get one thing perfectly clear: I am not a doctor. I don't even like going for a checkup, for that matter. So the last thing I'm going to do is delve into the science of the brain. You're welcome, by the way.

To be totally honest, I have no clue if there's a correlation between watching MMA and increased aggression. Although, I have to admit, this argument sounds eerily familiar. In my day, it was Marilyn Manson and Call of Duty that got a bum rap for all that is wrong with today's youth, but that's neither here nor there.

No, what I am is a sports writer for a major Canadian newspaper, who has covered firsthand a wide range of professional contact sports, including MMA. And based on my experiences, UFC is no more violent to watch or participate in than hockey, rugby, or football.

If you'll notice, boxing was left out of the mix. That's because MMA is in fact safer than the sweet science, at least according to a study by some dude named Johns Hopkins. I'm kidding; I know it's a university, and a very prestigious one at that.

Anyway, the researchers found that "the injury rate in MMA competitions is compatible with other combat sports involving striking. The lower knockout rates in MMA compared to boxing may help prevent brain injury in MMA events."

Basically, it's a fancy way of saying MMA may have a lot of blood and broken bones, but repeated head trauma is not part of the equation.

Okay, enough with nerd stuff. Let's talk about the fan experience. Well, as it turns out, you're safer attending an UFC event than a baseball game.

Let's take UFC 129, where a record 55 000 fans were on hand to watch Georges St.-Pierre defeat Jake Shields at Toronto's Rogers Centre on April 24, 2011. Despite being the organization's first foray into Canada's largest city, Toronto police said there were no arrests and no major incidents at the MMA show. To go one further, the average opening day for the Toronto Blue Jays, historically, gets more out of hand.

But back to ownership for a second. Chances are good you've heard of Dana White. Both profane and brash, White is the one person most responsible for transforming the image of the once-controversial spectacle of cage fighting into the more palatable sport of MMA.

Georges St.-Pierre lands a punch on Jake Shields at UFC 129 in Toronto.

As the president of UFC, not to mention a minority stakeholder, White has spent countless hours and hundreds of thousands of dollars of the organization's money lobbying to bring the sport to fight fans in North America and around the globe. And his hard work is paying dividends. Where once MMA was banned in almost every province and state, New York is the lone holdout as of 2012.

White's secret? That's easy. Educating the naysayers about MMA.

You see, most people who oppose MMA have never even bothered to watch the UFC. Nor have they invested any time in getting to know its athletes, nor taken the trouble to understand the vast nuances and complexities of the sport. Rather, they choose to play a game of connect the dots, with no more than their personal biases and few select medical journals to stand on.

Now touch gloves and let's have a clean fight …

What Inspires Me to Write

"Reading never came easy for me. A speech impediment made it almost impossible to read aloud and for whatever reason, sentences seemed jumbled and just didn't make sense. Then I discovered George Plimpton. *Open Net* is the first book I can remember reading from front to back. I was in Grade Six and just couldn't put it down. Yes, that meant it took me a while, but Plimpton's story about convincing the Boston Bruins to let him attend training camp and share his experiences of playing goal appealed to me so greatly that I chose to miss recesses to work through my problems. Looking back, that book would be one of the biggest influences in my career.

Not everything you're going to read is easy. But if you keep with it, I believe there's a book out there that will change your life too."

After

1. **Reading for Meaning** The essay "Fight Night" warns of the dangers of watching the UFC, whereas "Let's Have a Clean Fight" promotes the UFC.
    a) Reread each essay. As you read, list the evidence that each author used to support his or her argument in a T-chart.

Fight Night	Let's Have a Clean Fight

    b) Use the information you gathered in part (a) to help you summarize each author's argument.

2. **Understanding Form and Style**
    a) Compare and contrast the writing style of each author. Think about their tone, diction, and the types of evidence they use.
    b) Do you feel their writing styles affect how persuasive their arguments are? Why or why not?

3. **Student Voice** Identify one statement made by each author that you either agree with or disagree with. Explain why you agree or disagree.

4. **Speaking and Listening** Have a class debate, with one group arguing that UFC should be legal in Canada and the other group arguing that it should not be legal. In your debate, use information from these articles as well as any prior knowledge that you may have. Listen critically to the other group's arguments to develop effective counterarguments.

5. **Critical Literacy** Reread the author's short biographies at the beginning of each article. What do you know about these authors that may have affected the arguments they chose and the way they presented their arguments?

6. **Metacognition** How did your prior knowledge and opinion about the UFC affect how you read these essays? For example, were you willing to consider evidence that opposed your opinion about the UFC? If you did not have any prior knowledge about the UFC, how did this affect your understanding and feelings about the arguments the authors made?

Beyond

1. **Creating Media Texts** Create a video, brochure, or multimedia presentation promoting the skill involved in the UFC, or warning of the dangers of the UFC. Use information from these essays to make your promotional material as effective as possible.

2. **Reading for Meaning** Do additional research on the effects of watching violent sports, television, and movies, and playing violent video games. Present your findings in a written report or an oral presentation.

Top Ten Recording Artists
Every High School Band Should Know About

List

Written by Marc LaFrance

Marc LaFrance has performed as a drummer and singer on over 100 albums. When not producing and writing for his own record label, Delinquent Records, Marc continues to play, sing, and travel internationally with Randy Bachman, Bachman & Turner, as well as his own bands, Cease & Desist and Atlantic Crossing. He currently lives in Vancouver, British Columbia.

Tips

semicolon (;): most commonly used to connect independent clauses and suggest a closer relationship between the clauses than a period does

independent clause: a group of words that has both a subject and a verb and that could stand alone as a sentence

inference: the meaning reached by a reader based on what the author states or implies as well as the reader's prior knowledge or experience

Before

Reflect on the title. How do you think reading about great Canadian recording artists would help today's high school bands?

During

Many of the recording artists in this top ten list have things in common. As you read, make notes about common qualities and actions these recording artists did that contributed to their success.

Recording Artist	Qualities	Actions

Growing up in Winnipeg in the early Sixties was an amazing time. My world changed when The Beatles performed on *The Ed Sullivan* Show on February 9, 1964. For me and thousands of others, it was a religious experience. The brilliance of their song writing and their distinct playing ability set a new standard in popular music.

I got my first break as a drummer performing with the band Musical Odyssey and touring the western Canadian circuit. Since then, I've continued to record, perform, or tour with various Canadian and international artists.

After more than forty years playing in the music business, I recommend that every high school band should know the following top ten Canadian recording artists. I've listed them in the order their careers began.

Oscar Peterson

Music Career: 1945–2007

Jazz pianist and composer Oscar Peterson is considered one of the greatest jazz pianists of all time. In a career that spanned six decades, he played countless concerts to audiences worldwide. In his early years, he would practise four to six hours a day. He was heavily influenced by jazz greats such as Nat "King" Cole and Art Tatum. He, in turn, had a major influence on other keyboard greats such as Dianna Krall. His technique was impeccable; his hands would fly over the piano keys, never losing sight of the melody. Oscar was never afraid to take chances, which is the ultimate challenge in jazz circles.

Buffy Sainte-Marie

Music Career: 1953–present

Buffy Sainte-Marie is a Cree singer-songwriter and social activist born in Qu'Appelle Valley, Saskatchewan, with a truly original vocal style and unusual vibrato. Her songs have been covered by famous artists such as Elvis Presley, Barbara Streisand, Neil Diamond, and Cher. Buffy spent the early part of her career touring and performing throughout the world. There is no better way to gain musical and business experience.

Leonard Cohen

Music Career: 1956–present

Leonard Cohen is a singer-songwriter, musician, poet, and novelist. He is probably one of the best songwriters in our time. He uses his vast life experiences to write lyrics on the human condition. His unique singing style suggests that a great song can be sung by a mediocre singer and be successful. A song such as "Hallelujah" stirs so many emotions it stands right up there with John Lennon's "Imagine." More than 2000 renditions of Cohen's songs, such as "Suzanne," "Dance Me to the End of Love," and "Closing Time," have been recorded around the world.

Neil Young

Music Career: 1960–present

Neil Young is a true legend. He's a singer-songwriter and musician who made the most of his talents. He cofounded the band Buffalo Springfield along with Stephen Stills and Richie Furay, and then joined Crosby, Stills, Nash & Young in 1969. Being part of these acts during a very creative time in popular music was not enough for Neil. As a solo artist, he became one of the most prolific songwriters and performers of our time. His genres include acoustic folk, country rock, and hard rock. Many consider him to be the "Godfather of Grunge." His vocals and guitar playing are rough around the edges but contribute to his original sound.

Joni Mitchell

Music Career: 1960–present

Joni Mitchell, a musician and singer-songwriter from Saskatchewan, began her career by touring constantly to develop her performance skills and craft. This touring got her recognized and her original songs were recorded by notable singers such as Buffy Sainte-Marie. Joni moved to Southern California, signed a record deal, and had her own hits in 1968 with "Big Yellow Taxi" and "Woodstock." She was an artist who wasn't afraid to take chances. She started to explore jazz and fused it with rock and more complex beats. Her extensive vocal range and open-tuned guitar compositions give her countless variations within her melodies.

The Guess Who

Music Career: 1965–present

The Guess Who, one of the first Canadian bands to make it big internationally, paved the way for many Canadian musicians. In 1970, they sold more records than The Beatles or The Rolling Stones. Their strength was in the song writing. The song-writing team of Randy Bachman and Burton Cummings crafted many of the band's best songs, such as "These Eyes," "No Sugar Tonight," "Laughing," and "American Woman." Randy Bachman's cutting-edge, overdriven guitar sound was brilliant. Burton Cummings' vocal style was very distinctive and always in pitch. Robert Plant from Led Zeppelin was a huge fan of Burton's singing. Garry Peterson's drumming had a jazz influence yet he implemented strong rock beats. And, of course, Jim Kale was solid on bass.

Anne Murray

Music Career: 1968–present

Anne Murray, a singer in pop, country, and adult contemporary styles, is considered a Canadian icon. She was the first Canadian woman to achieve international success and was a trailblazer for artists such as Céline Dion, Sarah McLachlan, and Shania Twain. Her smooth vocal style and the right song choices contributed to her success in the music business.

Her signature first hit, "Snowbird," is a great illustration of this winning combination. Her live performances have always been noted for her very strong singing and her charming onstage personality, making her the consummate performer.

Bryan Adams

Music Career: 1977–present

Rock singer-songwriter and musician Bryan Adams is one of the hardest-working artists in the business. In his early years, after a short stint with his first recording act, Sweeney Todd, he concentrated on writing songs with Jim Vallance, a world-class songwriter. Like the writing teams of Lennon–McCartney (of The Beatles) and Jagger–Richards (of The Rolling Stones), Adams and Vallance wrote many notable songs such as "Run to You" and "Summer of '69." Bryan has been known to work on his own album in one studio and run into the next studio to try to pitch his songs to another artist.

k.d. lang

Music Career: 1984–present

Singer-songwriter k.d. lang is said to "probably have the greatest voice in modern pop music." k.d's voice is like no other; her perfect pitch and expert back phrasing are captivating. k.d.'s live performances of Leonard Cohen's "Hallelujah" are the marriage of a great song with a superlative singer. She has won several Grammy awards for her vocal performances. Madonna once described k.d. as "Elvis is alive and she's beautiful."

Sarah McLachlan

Music Career: 1988–present

Sarah McLachlan, a singer-songwriter, is best known for her wonderfully moving ballads. Her beautiful lilting voice and vocal range are the perfect combination for this musical genre. Her song "Angel," an emotionally charged piece of music, contributed to the success of her album "Surfacing," making it number one on

the Billboard 100 album chart. Sarah is one of those few artists who does not need a full band; her pure and impeccable voice is the only thing she needs to accompany herself on the piano. She also helped to further the careers of other female musicians by founding Lilith Fair, a concert tour and travelling music festival that showcased female musicians.

What Inspires Me to Be a Musician

> I love playing music. As a drummer and singer, I am connected to the groove and the melody, and it is a great physical feeling. Playing off the other musicians is like a chemical reaction. I guess the biggest thrill about being a musician is when you get to experience the reaction of the audience when you are performing live. There's no life like it.

After

1. **Reading for Meaning**   Make inferences to explain what the author means when he says that hearing The Beatles on *The Ed Sullivan Show* in 1964 was a religious experience for him.

2. **Understanding Form and Style**   In addition to his own opinion, what types of evidence does the author include to support his argument that these artists are in the "top ten"?

3. **Student Voice**   This top ten list has been created by one person with his own perspective. What musicians are not on this list who you think should be? Why?

4. **Critical Literacy**   Look back to the notes you made for the During reading activity. Which qualities does the author most value and admire in musicians? Do you share those values when you select music to listen to?

5. **Metacognition**   Did reflecting on the title help you put the information in this selection into context? In other words, did it help you understand what the author was trying to communicate? Why or why not?

Beyond

1. **Speaking and Listening**   Choose one of the recording artists mentioned in this selection. Listen to a song that he or she has recorded. Think about what elements of the song (such as the melody, the lyrics, the guitar solo) speak to you. Play the song for the class and explain why it is powerful.

2. **Student Voice**   Using a format similar to this selection, explain the accomplishments of a recording artist you enjoy. Make sure to include examples of the musician's success and a supporting quotation.

Walking to His Own Beat:
An Interview with Joseph Lubinsky-Mast

Interview

Written by Karli Desrochers

Karli Desrochers is a nineteen-year-old from Edmonton, Alberta, with countless goals and aspirations. Due to a neuromuscular genetic condition called spinal muscular atrophy, she has limited mobility and uses an electric wheelchair; however, she doesn't let this define her in the slightest. Karli's most significant passion has always been music, which led her to an internship in the industry at age sixteen. She hopes to continue her path in the entertainment industry with the intention of spreading positive messages to as many people as possible.

Before

Preview this selection.
a) What text features indicate that this is an interview?
b) Based on the visuals that accompany this selection, what can you infer about the person being interviewed?

During

As you read the interview, make a list of questions you would like to ask this musician being interviewed.

Tips

infer: to conclude something based on facts and reasoning

paraphrase: restating an idea or text using your own words

i.e.,: abbreviation for the Latin term *id est*, which means *that is* or *in other words*

Joseph Lubinsky-Mast is a bassist from Edmonton, Alberta, currently residing in Vancouver, British Columbia. After completing a diploma in jazz performance at Grant MacEwan College, Joseph attended the Hugh Fraser Jazz Orchestra program at the Banff Centre with jazz great Chucho Valdez. Joseph's love for music has led him to perform a wide range of musical styles, including punk, rock 'n' roll, R&B, hip-hop, country, jazz, and blues. He has toured across Canada, the United States, and Europe. Currently, Joseph is touring with the bands Sumner Brothers and The British Columbians.

Can you start off by telling us how you ended up going to a high school for the performing arts and a bit about your experience there?

When I was finishing Grade Nine, I knew that music was something I had a passion for. I wasn't sure what path I wanted to take. After going to many open houses for high schools, what really sold me on the Victoria School of the Arts was the creative energy of the school. Also, there were more options available to someone interested in the arts than at any other high school.

My experience at Vic. was great. I appreciated the teachers as well as the inspired and open-minded students. They allowed me to ignore many of the pressures the average high school student deals with and really focus on my studies.

What was the pivotal moment when you knew that being a musician was the path you wanted to take?

I remember the first punk show I went to in Grade Eight. The energy that I felt among the kids at the show, the passion that the bands put into their performance, the sense of camaraderie between the bands and the crowd was something special. I knew I needed to be part of it.

How did your friends and family feel about you choosing this career?

I've been very lucky. I have had nothing but full support from everyone. My parents were both very musical; my mother was a singer and pianist, my father was a bassist and general music aficionado. They put a fiddle in my hands at age five. My brothers are all talented musicians. The fact that I knew most of my friends in high school and college through music meant that we all pushed each other musically.

What would you say was the most discouraging moment for you during high school? If you had the chance, what would you go back and tell yourself about this?

I think one of the toughest parts about Grade Twelve in particular is the idea that this is the year that can make or break your life's ambitions. I think kids put too much pressure on themselves to smarten up and figure out what they are going to do in life. I convinced myself that it was time to smarten up and play "grown-up music," to stop playing sports and punk music, and to focus on being a jazz/classical musician. I was definitely miserable ignoring things that I really enjoyed.

I would go back and tell myself that the time to make the decisions that will define my life is a long way off. High school is the time to take in, experience, and learn as much about life as possible.

What about the most encouraging moment?
I was lucky to have two great music teachers who expected high standards and pushed all of us to improve as much as possible. When you're starting out on an instrument, you notice your growth as a musician, and at times it's very encouraging.

I remember the band I was part of in high school. It was a lot of fun watching audiences grow from forty people to two hundred people. There were shows where the audience was going wild, and the energy I got from that would last for weeks.

Who or what are some of your past and current influences?
Everyone who I get to play music with has had an influence on me. But without doubt, the two most important influences in my life are my parents. They have shaped me to be a hard-working, patient yet tenacious, positive individual. Without their guidance, I probably wouldn't have picked up music or stuck with it the way I have.

In high school, I had a fantastic band teacher. He inspired me with his knowledge and passion for music as well as his high level of musicianship.

Throughout my last year in high school and college, I studied classical bass from a great mentor. His favourite saying was, "You don't know what you don't know!" He cared deeply for all his students and instilled in me a work ethic, skills, and a sense of humility. He inspired me to always strive for the next level of musicianship.

Can you tell us about life as a Canadian musician?
I think it's harder here than in other parts of the world. The distances between cities and low population density impacts the amount of travel necessary and provides one of the biggest obstacles for any artist. When I toured Europe, I

got a sense of the support for travelling acts and the arts in general. It is part of the culture there to go out and take in plays, exhibitions, and concerts.

Personally, it's not feasible for me to make a living playing solely original music yet. I have to stay diverse in what I do. I work with a few cover bands that provide me with a steady income. Even though it can feel like a grind at times, I feel that, long term, I am gaining skills that will carry me into the future. Plus, it's a great feeling playing Michael Jackson and Stevie Wonder covers to a packed dance floor at 2:00 in the morning!

Where do you see yourself in five years?

I've found Vancouver to be an inspiring city to live in. With that in mind, what I'm doing musically now is very different than what I had anticipated doing when I moved here three years ago. I would really like to maintain a diverse array of projects. I want to be playing on more original projects, and I would love to spend more time in the studio than I am now. Whatever I will have going on, I am sure it will be interesting.

Lastly, what would you like to say to the readers who would like to pursue more creative career paths such as yours?

Embrace every chance to play music. You can't take opportunities for granted and, more importantly, you can't make a habit of saying no. When I was five years old, playing fiddle, I never would have imagined being moved by punk rock. Musically, I'm doing things now that I would never have imagined when I fell in love with the bass guitar in Grade Eight. Everything I've done has led to new experiences, from joining a jazz band in high school to studying jazz in college to moving to a new city.

I don't believe that success is based solely on talent. It's based on work ethic and the mindset to fearlessly embrace new experiences.

What Inspires Me to Write

> For as long as I can remember, I have felt dedicated to and loved music as well as getting to know people. Music is something that follows you throughout your entire existence, no matter what life brings your way. Intended emotions of a song can be recognized when it's in another language (or purely instrumental), and music can be "felt" by those with hearing impairments. I feel it connects so many people because it is timeless and universal, which is absolutely beautiful. Every song out there evokes feelings in people, whether it's a handful of individuals or millions. Having the opportunity to directly connect with those behind this music is inspiring in itself. Furthermore, being a part of bridging the gap between the fans and the band members is something I'll always love to do.

After

1. **Reading for Meaning**   Paraphrase Joseph's answers to two questions. Focus on the key points he makes in his answers.

2. **Understanding Form and Style**   How is the information you get in an interview different from information found in other types of nonfiction texts?

3. **Student Voice**   Joseph states, "I don't believe that success is based solely on talent. It's based on work ethic and the mindset to fearlessly embrace new experiences." Do agree with his statement about success? Why or why not?

4. **Critical Literacy**   Reread Karli Desrochers' (the interviewer's) short biography and her Inspiration note. Why do you think she asked the questions that she did in this interview? Think about her background and goals, as well as the intended audience of this interview (i.e., you and your classmates).

5. **Metacognition**   How did paraphrasing Joseph's answers affect your understanding of his experiences and thoughts?

Beyond

Speaking and Listening   Conduct an interview with another student about his or her passion. Use the questions in this interview as models for your own questions. Listen carefully to the person you are interviewing and ask clarifying questions if you need to.

BY THE NUMBERS: CAR FACTS

Statistics

Written by Jeremy Cato

In twenty-plus years of covering the auto industry, Jeremy Cato has won more than two dozen journalism awards, including being named Automotive Journalist of the Year three times. Cato was born in Montreal and grew up in the San Francisco Bay Area. While he's proud of his graduate degree from the University of British Columbia, it was harder and certainly more dangerous to graduate from the Spenard-David School of Racing, the Skip Barber Racing School, and a number of other driving schools.

Tips

sentence fragment: often looks like a sentence, but does not contain a complete thought because either the subject or predicate is missing or incomplete. The information in this list is presented in point form, so it is made up almost entirely of sentence fragments.

abbreviation: a shortened form of a word or phrase. The author uses abbreviations for measurement terms (such as *km/h* for kilometre per hour and *s* for seconds) throughout this selection.

Before

Suppose an automotive expert is going to visit your class. Generate a list of questions you would like to ask this person about current car facts.

During

As you read, try to put the numbers and measurements into perspective by making connections to your personal experience and knowledge. For example, the fastest car can go 439 km/h. That's more than four times faster than I travel on the highway!

If you're becoming more knowledgeable about cars because you're either learning to drive or simply like cars, you might find these car facts interesting.

439 km/h: The top-tested speed of the world's fastest production car, the Bugatti Veyron Super Sport.

2.4 s: The number of seconds the Bugatti Veyron Super Sport car takes to zoom from 0 to 100 km/h.

The Bugatti Veyron Super Sport car.

$2.6 million (USD): The price of the Bugatti Veyron Super Sport car, which is the most expensive production car in the world.

140 km/h: The top speed of the Nissan LEAF, the world's first mass-produced pure electric vehicle.

$38 395: The price of the Nissan LEAF in Canada.

7 h: The number of hours to recharge the LEAF battery on a 240 volt station. It takes 18 h to recharge the battery on a normal household 110 volt outlet.

83%: The percentage of all vehicles sold in Canada powered solely by gasoline; 13.2% were so-called "flexible fuel vehicles" capable of running on ethanol.

193: The number of "new" vehicle model introductions in Canada in the past eleven years. More than one quarter of these models are now off the market and no longer for sale.

309 000 km: The number of kilometres expected for the useful life of a vehicle in Canada.

409 000 km: The number of kilometres expected for the useful life of a vehicle in the United States.

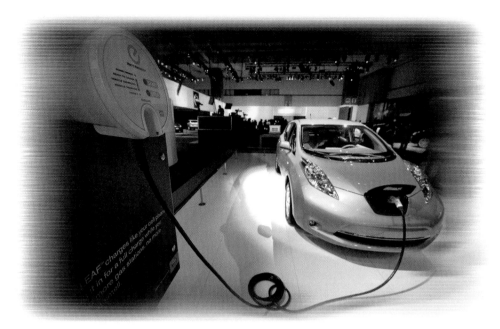
The Nissan LEAF plugged in to recharge its battery.

20 243 Km: The number of kilometres driven per vehicle in Canada last year.

20 207 Km: The number of kilometres driven per vehicle in the United States last year.

78.1%: The percentage of the driving-age population in Canada who own a vehicle.

96.4%: The percentage of the driving-age population in the United States who own a vehicle.

468 h: The average number of hours Canadians spend in their vehicle each year.

405 h: The average number of hours Americans spend in their vehicle each year.

What Inspires Me to Write

" The world is filled with fast cars, safer cars, high-paid auto-industry executives, consumer demands, and government regulators. Each influences what shows up in your local car dealership and each has an impact on employment in the auto industry. It's a fascinating world from every angle. "

After

1. **Reading for Meaning**   Why do you think the kilometres expected for the useful life of a vehicle in Canada are 100 000 less than in the United States?

2. **Understanding Form and Style**   Do you find the format of this selection an effective way to present information? Why or why not?

3. **Understanding Form and Style**   Which of the following statements is *not* a sentence fragment? Rewrite the other sentences so that they are no longer sentence fragments.
    A. The price of the Bugatti Veyron Super Sport car, which is the most expensive production car in the world.
    B. The number of kilometres driven per vehicle in Canada last year.
    C. More than one quarter of these models are now off the market and no longer for sale.
    D. The number of "new" vehicle model introductions in Canada in the past eleven years.

4. **Student Voice**   Do you think the car industry should focus on developing electric cars like the LEAF instead of cars that use gasoline? Why or why not?

5. **Critical Literacy**   What do you think the author was trying to get his readers to think about by presenting these facts? For example, what might these facts say about Canadian and American culture? What do they say about human nature?

6. **Metacognition**   Does having so many numbers in the article help or hinder your understanding of the information? Explain.

Beyond

1. **Reading for Meaning**   Research additional information about one of the following topics:
    - car usage in Canada and the United States
    - hybrid and electric cars
    - environmental impacts of driving a car versus using public transportation.

    Present your findings in a written report or multimedia presentation. Be sure to include charts and graphs to help people visualize the data.

2. **Speaking and Listening**   Considering the highest speed limit in Canada is 110 km/h, some people may argue that extremely fast cars, such as the Bugatti Veyron Super Sport car, should not be made. Have a class debate with one side arguing that cars like the Bugatti Veyron Super Sport car should not be made, and with the other side arguing that they should be made.

PROFILES OF ATHLETES AND PEOPLE IN SPORTS

Interview and Articles

By Maddie Porter

Maddie Porter is a Grade Twelve student in Thunder Bay, Ontario. She competed at the Canada Winter Games as a synchronized swimmer. She is a regular volunteer at her local homeless shelter. Maddie looks forward to attending university next year.

Before

Why would you read an interview or a profile of someone? What kind of information would you expect to get from reading this kind of text?

During

As you read about these athletes and people in sports, what do you wonder about them? What questions would you like to ask them?

Tips

profile: a short biographical text presenting a person's most noteworthy characteristics and achievements

quotation marks (" "): punctuation used at the beginning and end of a direct quotation; in the profile of Carol Huynh, quotation marks are used around words that Carol directly said; in the interview with Kyle Dubas, there are no quotation marks because the interview follows a convention where all the text after each question is directly from Kyle.

convention: a practice or device that is accepted as a necessary, useful, or given part of a genre; the interview with Kyle Dubas follows the convention of the interview genre where the question in bold is from the interviewer and the text that follows is directly from Kyle.

An Interview with Kyle Dubas

Kyle Dubas, 25, is the general manager of the Sault Ste. Marie Greyhounds Hockey Club. Kyle began working for the club at eleven years of age, becoming a scout with the club when he enrolled at Brock University at the age of seventeen. Upon turning twenty, Kyle became a player agent and became the youngest-ever NHLPA–certified player agent when he was twenty-two years old. Only a couple years later, Kyle was named the general manager of the Greyhounds.

What advice would you give to your fourteen-year-old self?

Life is about how you respond to adversity or challenges. That's where it is determined what you become in life. How do you respond when things don't go your way? Do you stand around and let disappointment crush you, or do you embrace adversity, attack it, and reach your potential?

When you became a scout at seventeen, where did you see your career in hockey going?

Quite honestly, when I was seventeen, scouting for the Soo Greyhounds and also doing class full-time at Brock, I aimed to become an NHL general manager. The goal I set for myself was to be at the very top of the vocation I was pursuing.

General Manager of the Soo Greyhounds (right) and Head Coach Mike Stapleton (left) signing hockey player Ryan Kirkup (middle).

Was there a specific moment when you knew you wanted a career in the business side of hockey?

That moment came when I was fifteen years old, in Grade Eleven, and Craig Hartsburg was hired as our general manager and head coach in Sault Ste. Marie. Working closely with Coach Hartsburg for that season was the tipping point. I learned so much and developed a strong passion for the hockey operations side of the business. I wanted to pursue it as a career.

How do you handle the criticism that comes with being a general manager?

Criticism doesn't bother me. You can't allow it to. You have to put your process in place and trust it. Do not let others try to influence your plan. Whether it is successful or not, you will always be able to sleep at night when you know you stayed true to yourself. Personally, I view it as part of the job to deflect criticism from coaches, players, and the organization. I'm completely confident in the process in place and it is no problem to deal with short-term criticism.

What are some of the advantages and disadvantages of being a general manager at such a young age?

The primary advantage to being in this position at a young age is that I have tremendous energy and enthusiasm. The job requires long hours and sometimes a lot of pressure so having that energy and enthusiasm are big benefits. On the personnel side, my age allows the players to feel more comfortable speaking with me and expressing issues or concerns.

The main disadvantage to being a general manager at only twenty-five is that people will attempt to discredit you based on your age. Whether it is the media or competitors, when they have nothing else to criticize you about, they automatically attack your age. The key is to just ignore it and work a little bit harder. You're always going to be proving people wrong, so you may as well get used to it and become great at it.

Who has had the greatest influence on your success?

My grandfather, Walter Dubas, coached the Greyhounds from 1965 to 1970, and he taught me so much about the importance of character and work ethic. Without those lessons, I would not be where I am today.

On the hockey side of things, he taught me the importance of building teams from the "back-end" (goaltenders and defence) out. His teams were always tough to play against and he always defended his players. To him, it was about the players. He was there to help and develop them. Sometimes, that's something people in hockey forget. We are all here to develop the players.

What words of wisdom do you have for young people looking to make an impact early on in their careers?

You need to get out and get involved. Volunteer early and as much as humanly possible. Work hard, don't expect much in return, and begin to make a name for yourself. In sports, like in other fields, you need to make yourself indispensable.

What are your goals for the future?

For my career, my goal is to become an NHL general manager and to build a club that can one day win a Stanley Cup. My larger goals are to lead a life of character and serve as a strong mentor for the players on our clubs and for others in the community. Most importantly, I never will forget where I came from and will stay true to my beliefs.

A Profile of Carol Huynh

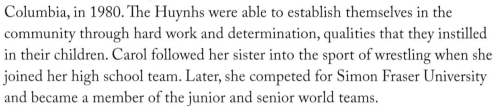

Carol Huynh always had a great competitive drive. She ran, she cycled, she was involved in many sports. But when she got into wrestling at age fifteen, she didn't expect it to lead her to the Olympic podium. Nevertheless, in 2008, the world watched her receive a gold medal at the Games in Beijing.

Carol is the daughter of two Vietnamese refugees who fled their home country and landed with little money in Hazelton, British Columbia, in 1980. The Huynhs were able to establish themselves in the community through hard work and determination, qualities that they instilled in their children. Carol followed her sister into the sport of wrestling when she joined her high school team. Later, she competed for Simon Fraser University and became a member of the junior and senior world teams.

From an early point in her career, Carol's coaches recognized her speed and agility as skills that would make her highly successful, but Carol credits her success to her ability to not take herself too seriously. She says the characteristics that helped her be successful in life and in sport are "a sense of humour, a competitive nature that motivates me to be my best, and a willingness and determination to work hard towards my goals."

Carol set her sights on the Olympics in 2002, when it was first announced that women's wrestling would be an Olympic sport. But setting the goal was the easy part; she faced many obstacles on the way to achieving her dream. At the trials for the 2004 games in Athens, Carol lost the final round to her teammate Lyndsay Belisle, and was forced to give up her spot on the Olympic team. Carol refers to the loss as "a wake-up call that highlighted the many things I needed to work on in order to pursue my dream of competing for Canada at the Olympics."

In 2006, she moved from Vancouver to Calgary. She left behind the wrestling club that had been her home and family for eight years in search of improved coaching and training. Despite these challenges, Carol maintains that the biggest obstacle she had to tackle was her self-confidence: "Wrestling is an individual, high-pressure, combative sport. I was crumbling in high-pressure competitive situations and not reaching my potential. I really worked hard on my confidence leading up to the Olympic trials and the Games, which contributed in large part to my success there. Confidence is something I work on continuously."

Two years later, in Beijing, all of Carol's efforts paid off. She says the highest point of her career was those Olympic Games: "Winning a gold medal at such a huge event was the culmination of a dream I had pursued for so many years. It was absolutely amazing to have my family and friends watching from the arena and around the world."

Perhaps what is most amazing about Carol is that, throughout her years of training, she has managed to maintain balance in her life outside the arena. In high school, she played in her school band, excelled academically, and had an active family and social life. After graduating, she earned a BA in Psychology at Simon Fraser, and is now working towards her master's degree in counselling psychology. She has goals to become a sport psychologist and a high-level coach. The 2008 Olympics were not the end of her competitive career either; she continues to train for the upcoming Olympics.

Her ambitious goals could be attributed to what she has learned about life through her sport: "Striving to achieve something is achievement in itself. The journey is more important than the destination, because the destination is fluid and ever changing. Our perceptions or the way we interpret what is going on in our lives has a huge impact on the way we feel about ourselves and what we are doing. If you can learn to perceive things in a more positive and helpful way, the happier you will be, and I think that's a success!"

Carol has proved that, with the right attitude, no opponent is impossible to beat, no obstacle is impossible to overcome, and no goal is impossible to achieve.

A Profile of Rubin Carter

Imagine you were sent to jail for twenty years of your life for something you didn't do. Could you say you were grateful for the experience? That's what Rubin Carter says. You might know him as Rubin "Hurricane" Carter, a boxer, known for his quick fists and explosive, knockout punches. At the height of his boxing career, Carter was sent to jail. But it was his mental toughness, more than physical prowess, that got him out.

Carter grew up in Patterson, New Jersey, an area known for its deep divide between the white and black communities. As a boy, Carter was violent and troubled. He did not have a lot going for him. He had a speech impediment that made his peers and teachers perceive him as stupid. Carter was first arrested at age twelve, after attacking a man he believed was a pedophile taking advantage of his friend. Carter was sent to a reform school for boys. In 1954, after nearly six years in the reformatory, Carter ran away and joined the military.

Rubin Carter (right) knocking out Florentino Fernandez in the first round of a fight in 1962 at Madison Square Gardens, New York.

While serving as a paratrooper, Carter first developed an interest in boxing. He says in his book, *Eye of the Hurricane*, that he first became a boxer because he could not speak and boxing was a means of expression.

Expressing himself with his fists resulted in two European lightweight titles while Carter served in the military overseas, and he returned to New Jersey with plans to become a professional boxer. Unfortunately, as soon as he got back, Carter was arrested for his escape from the reform school and taken to Trenton State Prison. In the following years, Carter was arrested several more times and sentenced to more jail time.

During those years, Carter continued to channel his anger into boxing. He turned professional in 1964. He also became a strong advocate against police brutality in the African-American community. But more trouble lay ahead. Carter's criminal record and his advocacy work put him at odds with the police.

At the height of his boxing career, Carter and another black man were arrested for the murder of three patrons in a bar. They fit the eyewitness description of "two Negros in a white car." A jury of twelve white people found the two guilty, based on two unreliable eyewitnesses and some manufactured evidence. Rubin Carter and his acquaintance, John Artis, were sentenced to three lifetime prison terms.

Carter maintained his innocence throughout his time in jail. He refused to shave his beard. He refused to wear a prisoner uniform. He refused to eat prison food. Because of his defiance, Carter spent nearly ten of his twenty years in prison in solitary confinement. While in prison, Carter wrote his first book, an autobiography called *The Sixteenth Round*. He also became an expert in criminal law, an amazing accomplishment for someone who had only a Grade Eight education. But Carter was determined to prove his innocence. When his book was published, it was sent to Nelson Mandela, Muhammad Ali, Aretha Franklin, and Stevie Wonder. Bob Dylan even wrote a song entitled *Hurricane*, all in the hopes that media attention would set Rubin Carter free.

And it did, but only for six months. Carter was found guilty for a second time. Returning to prison was Carter's lowest point. But although he was physically imprisoned, he didn't allow himself to be mentally or spiritually restrained. He was so determined to set himself free that he taught himself all the ins and outs of the judicial system that continued to fail him. He was later rewarded with two honorary law degrees for his efforts in educating himself.

After a decade and a half in prison, Carter received a letter from a boy named Lesra Martin who had read his autobiography. Martin was growing up in an impoverished area of New York when he met a group of Canadian entrepreneurs who saw his potential and wanted to help with his education. Carter and Martin began a correspondence. In 1983, Martin and his Canadian benefactors moved to New York with the goal of proving Carter's innocence. Through dedication, determination, and hard work, Carter was exonerated in 1985. The judge stated that Carter's "convictions were predicated upon an appeal to racism rather than reason, and concealment rather than disclosure."

Rubin Carter is now the CEO of Innocence International, an organization that helps free the wrongfully convicted. Throughout his life, Carter has transformed himself from a violent teenager to a prizefighter to an angry prisoner to a free man. He was able to free himself both physically and mentally. Against all odds, Carter has built a happy, healthy, and successful life for himself.

Carter states in his book that without going to prison, he might not have stopped long enough to truly discover who he is. He urges us to break free of whatever prison we are confined by, and gives the same message to all people regardless of their circumstances: "Dare to dream."

What Inspires Me to Write

> *Writing isn't always my favourite thing to do. When I do make time for it, it helps me to sort out all the crazy thoughts in my head.*

After

1. **Reading for Meaning** Which person used sports as a vehicle to focus his or her negative behaviour and difficulties growing up? Choose the best answer below.
   A. Kyle Dubas
   B. Carol Huynh
   C. Rubin Carter
   D. All of the above

2. **Understanding Form and Style** Which form did you feel best expressed information about the athletes: the interview of Kyle Dubas; the profile of Carol Huynh, which included quotations from Carol; or the profile of Rubin Carter? Use examples from the text to support your opinion.

3. **Speaking and Listening** In a small group, discuss how the content and format of these three profiles are similar and how are they different. Use a chart or Venn diagram to record your group's ideas.

4. **Viewing and Representing** Choose one of profiles that you found inspirational. Write a short inspirational message based on something in that profile. Design a bumper sticker with that message. Keep in mind your bumper sticker should quickly make an impact on people who see it.

5. **Student Voice** Becoming a world-class athlete requires countless hours of training. Often, these athletes have to sacrifice other parts of their life, such as their social life and schooling, to pursue their dreams in sports. Would you make these same sacrifices to pursue your dream—whatever that may be? Explain why or why not.

6. **Critical Literacy** All three of these sports figures overcame some level of adversity to find success.
   a) By focusing on the positive side of their stories, what message is the author sending to students who might want to get involved in professional sports?
   b) How would these profiles be different if they'd been written by an author who wanted to discourage students from going into sports?

7. **Metacognition** As you read, did you ask yourself whether you understood what you were reading? If you did not understand, did you ask yourself why? How do these questions help you to understand what you are reading?

Beyond

1. **Creating Media Texts** Design a booklet, Web page, blog posting, or multi-media presentation about five "rules to live by" that will help someone be successful in life. Add visuals to make your points.

2. **Student Voice** Create a set of interview questions you would like to ask someone whom you consider to be successful in some way. Explain a bit about this individual and why you chose this person.

COOL SCHOOLS

Article

Written by Wilbur McLean

Wilbur McLean has been writing professionally for more than ten years. An award-winning former journalist whose work has appeared in more than ten different Canadian newspapers, he now works full-time in the public sector as a communicator. He currently lives in Medicine Hat, Alberta, and always enjoys a riveting game of Scrabble.

Tips

initialism: an abbreviation formed using the first letter or letters of each word in a phrase or name; for example, *NSS* is an initialism for *National Sport School*; initialisms are often called acronyms, although an acronym should technically form a pronounceable word, such as the acronym *radar* for *radio detecting and ranging*.

quotation: a passage of text or speech that is repeated by someone other than the original author or speaker

proposal: a plan or suggestion put forward for consideration or discussion by others

Before

This article is about high schools that offer programs to meet students' unique needs, interests, and goals. Read this article with the purpose of learning about these programs and thinking about new programs your school or community might be able to offer.

During

As you read, make connections to your own experiences in high school and how they are different than or similar to the students interviewed in this article.

School: Stelly's Secondary School
Location: Saanichton, British Columbia
Program: Boulder's Climbing Academy
Grades: 9 to 12

The Boulder's Climbing Academy is helping Grade Twelve student Alison Stewart-Patterson climb higher every day, both literally and figuratively.

Stewart-Patterson is a native of Kamloops, British Columbia, but is enrolled at Stelly's Secondary School's climbing academy. The two are separated by 450 kilometres and the Strait of Georgia but Stewart-Patterson made the switch for exactly one reason.

Alison Stewart-Patterson climbing the wall at Boulder's Climbing Academy.

"I love climbing. I've been doing it since I could walk," she says. Stewart-Patterson is a national-level climber who has competed in the World Youth Climbing Championships four times.

At Boulder's Climbing Academy, students can enroll in two elective, Grade Twelve–level courses that find students engaged in climbing activities in Boulder's 1200 square metres of climbing terrain. Heavily involved students take their participation to another level by volunteering with Boulder's, including assisting with the design and planned operation of a new addition to the facility, which made Boulder's the first world-class climbing facility in the country.

For Stewart-Patterson, it has added up to a school experience unlike anything she had previously known.

"It's definitely changed my perspective. I always have a class every day that's also the sport I love," she says.

School: Centennial Collegiate Vocational Institute
Location: Guelph, Ontario
Program: Community Environmental Leadership Program
Grades: 10 and 12

For an entire semester, students enrolled in the Community Environmental Leadership Program (CELP) leave behind their brick-and-mortar schools and are bussed twenty minutes to Camp Edgewood. While there, students learn through experiencing the outdoors. They develop a relationship with nature and earn a respect for the importance of environmental sustainability.

CELP students canoeing at Camp Edgewood.

"It lives up to its name in terms of community building," says Anna Vanderkooy, who completed both the Grade Ten and Grade Twelve portions of the program.

Vanderkooy says she most enjoyed the nontraditional aspects of the program that allowed students to learn through experience.

"It's really based on experiential learning, which can be missing from some people's education," she says.

Some of the highlights for Vanderkooy included wilderness and canoeing trips, working as mentors with Grade Five students, and starting a community garden.

"It was one of the most fulfilling experiences of my life," says Vanderkooy, now twenty-two and completing her Environmental Studies degree at the University of Waterloo.

As part of the program, students also learn about local environmental issues and cook for their class on a regular basis.

"The teachers provided us with so much trust. We had a lot of freedom to really explore the areas that interested us and were given opportunities to develop our own interests," concluded Vanderkooy.

School: Victoria School of the Arts
Location: Edmonton, Alberta
Program: Fine arts school
Grades: Kindergarten to Grade 12

Young artists in Edmonton know where they want to go to school to thrive in an environment with like-minded students: Victoria School of the Arts.

Former student Alex Saavedra feels that the personalities at Victoria make the school experience worthwhile.

"Everyone had their own character and just about everyone was a friend," says Saavedra. "No matter who you are, you will be accepted there."

Students at Victoria sing, dance, draw, paint, and perform in an arts-focused education that begins in kindergarten and continues all the way through until high school graduation.

A list of extracurricular activities at Victoria reads like an arts festival, as student performances and exhibitions occur on an almost weekly basis, producing an exceptionally tight-knit school–community relationship.

Saavedra sampled a number of different streams at Victoria. He started in the music program, shifted to photography, and then went with the graphic design stream.

"The level of detail and the things we learned were incredible," said Saavedra.

Canadian pop singer Kreesha Turner counts herself among former students of Victoria. Turner was nominated for numerous Juno awards for her debut album in 2008.

School: Nutana Collegiate
Location: Saskatoon, Saskatchewan
Program: Academy of Tourism
Grades: 9 to 12

Melissa Rabbitskin's circumstances made her an excellent fit for Nutana Collegiate's Canadian Association of Travel and Tourism (CATT) certification program.

Having given birth to a child as a young teenager, Rabbitskin continued her education but needed practical skills that would help her provide for her young child. CATT certification proved a perfect fit.

"I don't know how I would have been able to find a job after high school without it," says Rabbitskin.

Students at Nutana can take two CATT certification courses. Completing both courses awards students with a gold-level certification from CATT. The courses are hands-on as students plan school and community events, work on their service industry skills, and even receive first aid and CPR training.

"You can really break off into any part of tourism when you're done," says Rabbitskin, who spent time working at a hotel front desk upon completing the program. "I really got an appreciation for the world and for all the things tourism can offer."

In fact, Rabbitskin was inspired by the tourism program to travel upon completing her high school education. She spent most of a year after graduating visiting Mexico; Washington, DC; and Ottawa.

"When you're out in the world, you really know how service should be," she says. "It's so valuable."

School: National Sport School
Location: Calgary, Alberta
Program: Sports-focused education for Olympic-calibre athletes
Grades: 9 to 12

When a high school is connected to a bobsled run, ski-jumping facility, speed skating track, and Canada's Sports Hall of Fame, it's not difficult to figure out that it's a different kind of school.

The National Sport School (NSS) is the high school home for many of Canada's elite athletes in a variety of sports ranging from hockey to skiing to more unique disciplines such as equestrian, which is the specialty of Grade Eleven student Brigitte McDonald.

The ability to have a healthy balance between her athletic aspirations and educational requirements is what makes NSS a great school for McDonald.

"It's very flexible. If I go away for a competition or for training, I can catch up on my assignments easily," says McDonald.

Kaillie Humphries (shown with her bobsled partner Heather Moyse) is a former student of National Sport School. She won the gold medal in two-woman bobsled at the 2010 Winter Olympics.

NSS accommodates for its elite athletes by instituting flexible assignment due dates and test writing options. Each student also has forty-five-minute tutorial blocks each day to allow for personalized instruction that helps make up for times when students may miss class.

"It's really helpful," notes McDonald. "The school does lots to make sure we can be successful."

And success for NSS students has come on an international stage. In fact, twenty-one former NSS students competed for Team Canada at the 2010 Winter Olympics in Vancouver, and the school lists ten former students as having won an Olympic or Paralympic medal at some point.

What Inspires Me to Write

> I'm inspired to write by the possibilities writing presents. Unhappy with the service received? Write a letter of complaint. Miss a distant friend? Write an e-mail. Unsure what decision to make? Write the pros and cons. Feeling creative? Write a poem. Writing represents one of the most simple, yet powerful tools for anybody who chooses to utilize it. I write because I can.

After

1. **Reading for Meaning** What do the schools mentioned in this article have in common?
2. **Understanding Form and Style** The author provided several quotations from students who attend these schools. What effect do these quotations have on your understanding of and engagement with the article? Why do you think that is the case?
3. **Student Voice** Which of these high school programs interests you the most? Why?
4. **Viewing and Representing** Create a symbol or emblem for one of the schools you read about. The symbol should represent the most important characteristics of the school.
5. **Critical Literacy** In choosing these particular schools to write about, what values does the author seem to hold about an ideal education?
6. **Metacognition** How did making connections to your own high school experience and thinking about how you could improve that experience help you to engage with and understand this article?

Beyond

Student Voice What type of program could your school offer that would help you meet your current needs, interests, and/or goals? Write a proposal for this program for your school to consider.

Memoirs and Personal Reflections

BIG IDEA ›

How do we learn about ourselves when we read the reflections and memoirs of other people?

What are memoirs and personal reflections?

Memoirs focus on a portion of the author's life. Personal reflections are also about the author's experiences and feelings, but are less focused on the events in his or her life. Reading about another person's experiences can help you to gain perspective on issues and possibly rethink or strengthen your own opinions. In this section, you will read about adult writers' experiences as students, as well as the experiences of student writers.

How do I read memoirs and personal reflections?

> **Make connections**—As you read, make connections to your own experiences, other texts you have read, and your knowledge of the world around you. These connections can enrich your appreciation of the text.

> **Question and assess the author's perspective**—Memoirs and personal reflections are intensely personal and are written from the first-person point of view. Consider what values are present in the text, and how the author's background, biases, and opinions may shape what he or she writes.

The Dream Snatcher

Memoir

Written by trey anthony

trey anthony is the cocreator and executive producer of the TV series *'da Kink in my Hair*. She is a published playwright and has written for the Comedy Network and CTV, and worked on *The Chris Rock Show*. trey grew up in Rexdale, Ontario, in a housing complex, and moved to Brampton, Ontario, in her teen years. In her spare time, she enjoys pushing boundaries, questioning and redefining "the rules," and giving voice to those not often heard.

Tip

voice: conveys the attitude, tone, and thought patterns of the narrator or speaker in writing. Often readers make the mistake of assuming the voice of the narrator is the voice of the author, but in this case, it is not an error; trey anthony is the narrator and speaks strongly about her experiences.

Before

This selection is about how the author's abilities were underestimated in high school, but she turned out to be successful writer, actor, and TV producer. How might you, as a high school student, benefit from reading her story?

During

As you read, pay attention to how the author's attitude towards Miss B changes. Make connections to your attitude towards adults in your life and how those attitudes may have changed.

When you write the story of your life, make sure you are holding the pen.

—Author unknown

Sometimes I have this burning desire to find her. I have thoughts about looking her up. I want to Google her. I want to invite her to one of my shows, perhaps send her a newspaper clipping. Maybe one day, I will invite her to lunch, so I will finally get the chance to say, "It's not right, nor is it okay for you to shatter someone's dreams. And Miss, you were so wrong about me!"

I remember her clearly: my Grade Twelve advanced English teacher. Let's call her Miss B. She had a reputation for being a strict, no-nonsense, dry, frank, straight-talker. She was feared as much as she was hated. Most kids assigned to her class would immediately head to the guidance office, pleading to switch classes. Yet I was dying to be in her class because she taught the only novella-writing course in the school.

I was seventeen years old and my dream was to be a writer and an actor. I had so much I wanted to say and share, and was eager to impress her with my writing abilities and my vivid imagination. I was eager to write down the words, which felt like they were trying to take over my head. I wanted to learn as much as I could about writing, and viewed this class as the first major step towards becoming a "real" writer. My fingers were itching to write a fifty-page novella!

The first day of class, I looked around at the other students. I wasn't surprised to see that I was the only black girl in a sea of white faces. Many of the students of colour were streamed into the general classes or encouraged to take industrial classes such as woodworking, hairdressing, or mechanics. However, there was a South Asian girl who sat on the other side of the room. Every time I tried to make eye contact or smile, she averted her eyes, and pushed her glasses down to the tip of her nose and became engrossed with picking the red nail polish off her right thumb. I correctly concluded that we would never be friends.

Miss B sternly addressed the class, and listed her expectations and her impressive credentials. She was not only a creative literature teacher, but also a published writer who had won the fourth-place runner-up in a *Reader's Digest* writing competition *and* been published in the Brampton community newspaper! Thus, she stated proudly, she knew good writing when she saw it. She asked which of us wanted to be writers. I immediately raised my hand, alongside three of my classmates. Miss B shot a disappointed look at those who hadn't bothered to raise their hands, and slowly shook her head.

I immediately sympathized with her. How sad to be so talented and be stuck with a bunch of losers who didn't really want to write. I decided I would wow her, and perhaps she would send in my writing to *Reader's Digest* and I too could win a prize! I vowed to never let Miss B down. I would write as if my life depended on it!

But I did let her down. As much as I tried, I was a constant failure. Every assignment I handed in was promptly returned with a bloodbath of red marks all over it. I never got higher than a C+. One day after class I finally found the courage to approach her. I walked up to her desk, palms sweaty and heart pounding against my chest. I swallowed. I knew Miss B saw me, but she did not acknowledge me. I waited for a few minutes, then cleared my throat.

"Umm, Miss B, can I talk to you for a minute?"

"Yes," she responded, without looking up.

"I wanted to talk to you about my marks. I'm not sure why I'm getting the marks that I'm getting. How come I'm always failing everything?"

Miss B continued to mark her stack of papers, and said: "As far as I know, you're not failing, trey."

"Yeah, but I'm getting Cs. I want to do better. I really want to be a writer! I've always dreamt about being a writer. I want to write a book or maybe for a television show!" I nervously bit on my lower lip. Maybe I had said too much? But I wanted her to know that I was serious, not like the other losers—I mean students. I wasn't just taking the course for a credit. I anxiously awaited her response. "Miss, I really want to be a writer …" I silently begged her to just glance at me.

Miss B finally looked up from her papers and offered me a fake strained smile, the kind of smile you would offer a small child who says she is going to grow wings and fly to the moon. She looked directly into my eyes before slowly saying: "trey, you could never be a writer; your grammar is terrible. You write how you speak. I'm surprised that you even got into this advanced English class. And to be brutally honest, I don't think you have what it takes. Have you ever thought about being a hairdresser? Your hair always looks so nice."

I have struggled for many years to recall what my response was, and have desperately tried to remember how the conversation ended. But I truly can't remember. That memory is buried deep within me, in a place where dreams go to die.

Yet what I do know is that, the very next day, I went to the guidance office, dropped my advanced English literature class, and enrolled in Parenting 10l, where I carried an egg ("baby") in a basket around for two months. I decided I was better equipped to ensure the safety of an egg in a damn basket than write an English paper. I vowed that I wouldn't leave my precious egg on the school bus, and forced myself to forget all the words that desperately wanted to spill out onto the page. I had no time to dream about writing when I had an egg to take care of!

I never went back to Miss B's class. Every time I thought about writing, I would see her face, hear her words. I knew she was right, I was never going to be a "real" writer, but I did continue to write in secret. I kept countless journals, scribbled down my pain and all my private thoughts and dreams. Yet every time I thought about my dream, I quickly dismissed it and swallowed the burning shame within me. Someone like me could never be a writer.

For nearly nine years of my life, I never shared anything I wrote. Miss B's words continued to haunt me, and sometimes even now, when I become

frustrated with my work, or I've missed writing deadlines, or my editor sends me a list of things that I need to rewrite, or writer's block hits me, I sometimes hear her saying: "trey, you could never be a writer."

That is why I often feel this urge to look her up and yell, "You were wrong about me! I'm an award-winning writer! I'm the first African-Canadian woman to have her own show on a prime-time network! A television show that I cowrote and executive produced! My work is now read in schools, colleges, and universities, and presented on worldwide stages. Miss B, you need to Google me!"

But what I really want to do is invite Miss B to one of my opening nights, filled to capacity by black and brown faces hungry to hear our stories on stage, and see our images on television. I need her to know that she was wrong.

Deep down inside, I know she is not the person to blame. Yes, what she said to me was wrong, but the person most wrong was *me*, because for nine years of my life, I believed her. I believed that someone like *me* couldn't be a writer. I willingly gave her the power to take away my dreams. I believed in her words more than I believed in myself. It took me nearly nine years to find my own voice, to rediscover my dream, to begin to write again. It was nine whole years before I would step on stage and read and share my work publicly. Nine years to allow myself to dream again.

And now I'm here. Writing, acting, producing, writing, dreaming, writing. I'm just a simple black girl with a big dream! A dream that came true.

What Inspired Me to Write This Selection

> " I feel my biggest purpose in life is to be a voice for those who are not often heard and seen authentically. I'm passionate about engaging and speaking with youth, especially youth of colour and queer youth, and acknowledging their existence. I have witnessed firsthand how society tries to silence them and render them invisible or 'other.' My hope is that students who read this piece will be inspired to be defiant when the world tries to define them. "

After

1. **Reading for Meaning** Suggest reasons that the author focuses on Miss B as the main subject of this memoir.

2. **Understanding Form and Style** Miss B thought the author could never be a writer because she "writes how she speaks."
   a) Why might "writing how she speaks" have made her a successful writer?
   b) Do you think the author's voice makes this memoir easy or difficult to connect to? Explain.

3. **Speaking and Listening** In a small group, discuss how the author reacted to Miss B's assessment of her abilities. Discuss whether or not you would have dealt with the situation in the same way.

4. **Critical Literacy** Although the author's depiction of Miss B is negative, is it possible that Miss B had a positive impact on the author? Explain.

5. **Student Voice** How important a role do you think adults play in teenagers' success in school and in life in general?

6. **Critical Literacy**
   a) In what ways does the author feel her identity as a black person affected her experience in school and her success in her career?
   b) How might Miss B respond to the author's view of her experiences in school?

7. **Metacognition** How did making connections to your own life help you relate to and understand the author's experiences?

Beyond

Student Voice Imagine you have attained whatever your definition of success is in the future. Present this vision of success in the form of a magazine article or Web page about this future you, or a journal entry or Twitter feed by this future you.

Why I Can't Have Normal Friends

Personal Reflection

Written by Cade Bengert

Cade Bengert is in his final year of high school in Stettler, Alberta. He has a black belt in tae kwon do and was a silver medalist at the World Tae Kwon Do Championships in Telford, England. Cade loves writing songs, poetry, and short stories, and he is highly involved in theatre and film at his school. He is currently working on a novel, which he hopes one day will be published. His career goal is to become an English teacher.

Tips

infer: to understand something based on what the author states or implies as well as your prior knowledge or experience

allusion: a brief reference, explicit or implicit, to a place, person, or event

Before

Consider the title of this selection. As a class, brainstorm specific questions about what it means to be "normal." For example, Does normal mean fitting in with the crowd? Does normal mean being average height and average weight?

During

The author uses images to provide concrete pictures for his ideas in this selection. As you read, visualize the images the author describes and think about how the images help you understand what he is saying.

Because, simply put, I am not normal. I have issues. I have insecurities. I have imperfections. I have complications. But these things are more than just impurities in the sea that is my life. Each of these stains on my shirt of identity is a part of me. Every scar is a signature of my document. Every fear is a landmark on my highway. Every pimple, a mountain on my landscape.

I do not embody perfection. I do not have perfect grades or perfect looks. I do not have perfect confidence. I do not have these, Sam-I-Am. But there is one thing at which perfect, I am. I am the best me the world has ever seen, or ever will see, because no one can be me quite like I can be. No one else walks like I do, talks like I do, or messes things up with quite the same intensity. I am perfect at being me.

And it was me, you see, that you once loved. It was me, you see, who you used to stare at when I wasn't looking. It was me, you see, who made you laugh, made you think, made you see the world in a new light, made you weep with compassion, made you shake with excitement, and made you look forward to waking up every day, ready for new moments.

I am not perfect, and I never will be. But I have had a profound impact on this world. I have planted a seed in you, and sat back, and watched while it grew. I have watched this seed turn into a magnificent tree. And while, one day, I may not be graced with the glorious shade of your leaves, I will never lose the dreams that each one of us has. I'm not perfect, but for a moment I made you forget that. It grew like gardens of Babylon. Like blood through my loving heart did run. I am not perfect. That's fine. I never claimed to be. But it took my imperfections to make you see.

Everyone has been put down, beat up, and made to frown. We have all been fat, ugly, dumb, not enough, made fun of, and felt numb. We've been without hope. We've been unable to cope.

We have all been the black man at the back of the bus, with his hands covering his face, wishing they could cover his race. Well I'm here to tell you that you can find home in this place.

We have all been the woman who was raped that day. The one society told: "Well maybe if you didn't dress that way ..." Well I'm here to say: "Forget that, men shouldn't act that way!"

We have all been the boy who went home and cut, the one who felt worthless no matter what. Well, I'm here to stand by your side and open those doors you thought were shut.

We have all been that gay man, the one nobody understands. Well, I'm here to tell you I would be proud to hold your hand.

Ladies and gentlemen, I am gay. I am black. I am a woman. And you bet, I have cut. If you have a problem with that, then you're out of luck.

I am perfect, and so is each of you. Those who disagree need a different point of view. 'Cause the flaws in their eyes are the reason for their lies, and the imperfections they see are the reasons we continue to breathe, and those names that we hear shall cause us no fear. For we are the underdogs, the part of the machine below the other cogs. But we will not rest until we are seen, the world will be in awe of all we have been.

Here are my laws to live by:

1. Do not kill the confidence of others. You don't know how long it took them to build it up.
2. Never steal the wind from beneath another's wings.
3. Love shall be treated as sacred, no matter who it is between.
4. Don't lie to your neighbours by telling them they are anything less than perfect.
5. When you look in the mirror, like what you see.

Obey my laws! If you don't, I will not execute you, I will probably just give you a hug, and not let go until you agree they're true. Never say you aren't perfect. Cause you are. You are the best you the world could ever hope for.

What Inspired Me to Write This Selection

> I have battled depression for the past four years, and have recently sought help for it. At the time I wrote this piece, I had just begun treatment. The purpose of this piece is to give support to others facing the same hardships, and to let them know that they are not alone. We are all perfect and beautiful in our own ways, and everyone needs to be reminded of that sometimes.

After

1. **Reading for Meaning**   The author writes, "Ladies and Gentlemen, I am gay. I am black. I am a woman. And you bet I have cut." Is this literally true? What can you infer the author means by this?

2. **Understanding Form and Style**   The author makes an allusion to the children's book *Green Eggs and Ham* by Dr. Seuss when he says, "I do not have these, Sam-I-Am." Why do you think he alludes to this book? Look up this book in a library, if you need to.

3. **Speaking and Listening**   Read this selection aloud. Notice how the author repeats certain words or phrases over and over again.
   a) Identify four of these repeated words or phrases.
   b) What effect does this repetition have? How does it help communicate the author's message?
   c) Do you think the repetition has more impact when the selection is read aloud? Why or why not?

4. **Viewing and Representing**   Choose a theme from this piece. Create a visual representation of that theme in a form of your choice (for example, a mind map, a computer-generated illustration, your own original art, etc.) and post it in the classroom. View your classmates' visuals and try to guess their chosen themes.

5. **Student Voice**   Do you agree with the author when he writes, "I am perfect, and so is each of you. Those who disagree need a different point of view"? Why or why not?

6. **Critical Literacy**   Who is the intended audience of this selection? Who would benefit most from reading it?

7. **Metacognition**   How did visualizing as you read this selection affect your understanding of the author's message? If this strategy did not work well for you, what comprehension strategy tends to work better for you?

Beyond

Creating Media Texts   The author states that he wrote this selection as part of his treatment for depression. Research ways for students to seek help for depression in your area. Present your findings in the form of an advertisement in a magazine or on the radio. Be sure to be sensitive to your target audience.

The Night Shift

Memoir

Written by Dianah Smith

Dianah Smith was born in St. Ann's, Jamaica, and raised in Ottawa, Ontario. She started writing in her early teens as a way to express emotions that weren't encouraged in her home. Writing continues to be a form of self-expression, self-discovery, and healing for her. She also writes to document her life and culture, and to leave a legacy for future generations.

Before

In this selection, the author recalls her experiences at a summer job. What would be your ideal summer job? What types of summer jobs would you *not* want to have? Why?

During

As you read this piece, think about the author's relationship with her father and try to make connections to your own relationship with a parent or guardian.

Tips

tone: the attitude that runs through an entire text. This may include the writer's attitude towards the subject and/or the audience.

pace: the speed at which an author tells a story

The summer I was sixteen, I worked with my dad cleaning a factory across the Ottawa River in Aylmer, Quebec. Although Dad lived with us, he was rarely home. Most nights he would phone the apartment to let me know he was on his way. He was always brief. At about ten o'clock I waited at the corner of Lees Avenue and Chapel Street, a few doors down from our apartment, for him to come pick me up.

There were four other people, all adults, who worked with us: Ali, Jean-Guy, Paul, and Sherona. Ali was an older Guyanese man with rotting yellow teeth. Dad, our supervisor, suspected that he was sneaking naps while he was supposed to be cleaning. Dad suspected this because he did the same thing.

Paul and Jean-Guy were francophone guys who lived in Hull. Jean-Guy wore tight jeans and was always pulling a comb out of his back pocket and swiping it through his feathered hair. Paul was a scrawny-looking guy who wore glasses with thick lenses that made him look like he was in a perpetual state of fear or amazement. Sherona was the only other female, a light-skinned woman with large shoulders and big gaps between her teeth where molars used to be. When she laughed, a big bank of bright pink gums was exposed.

They were a rag-tag crew. Ironically, Dad, who struggled to read a simple sentence, was the leader of this crew. Jean-Guy was a bully and thief. For all of his boasting and preening, like a peacock with his feathers laid flat, he was small and vulnerable. Paul was cowed by the slightest hint of conflict. With the exception of huge eyes behind his glasses, nothing about him was magnificent. Ali had been in Canada for most of his adult life. He lived in a rooming house, shared a bathroom with others on the same floor, and heated up cheap store-bought dal and roti on a hot plate in his room.

Sherona was different. She'd been in Canada for only five years, and there was still light in her eyes. For a while I thought she was Dad's mistress. He talked to her in a way he didn't talk to my mom: not romantically, but honestly. He seemed to confide in her and she didn't seem to make demands of him. He would leave her on the job and disappear for two or three hours without an explanation. She said nothing when he returned. She brought in home-cooked meals in big, round, orange Tupperware containers, warped from going into the microwave even though they weren't the microwaveable kind. She cooked ackee and saltfish, boiled dumplings, cabbage, corned beef and rice, and sometimes soup.

Dad was usually late picking me up. He would get Sherona and Ali first. Sherona had the only other seat in the front of the van beside Dad. The back seats had been taken out to make room for all the cleaning equipment: buffers, steam cleaners, push brooms, dust mops, mops, and pails with the wringers hooked on the side. There were large plastic bottles of floor cleaners, window cleaners, carpet shampoo, toilet bowl cleaners, old rags, and packages of new J Cloths. Ali and I would roll up our jackets and sit on the floor or turn over a bucket and create a makeshift seat. Dad would sometimes yell back at me to keep low, because anyone under eighteen was supposed to, by law, wear a seat belt.

The drive to the factory induced sleep. There was nothing to see in the darkness outside the van's windows. The streets were even more deserted after

we crossed over to the Quebec side. Every now and then, another car's bright headlights would startle us, and Dad would flick his headlights on and off, yelling: "Dim you lights, dim you lights!" and signalling to the passing car.

When we pulled into the deserted parking lot of the factory, which was big enough for us to get lost in—by accident or on purpose—there was one other car keeping vigil. Dad always parked beside the security guard's rusty Trans Am, and we began what always felt like a long walk to the entrance.

Our "lunch break" was at three-thirty in the morning. We ate in the cleaning staff office. The office was a large concrete room in the basement, with one desk and chair, a microwave, and a phone. The metal door locked with a padlock. Dad or Sherona sat on the chair at the table. Sometimes they offered their seat to me. The others used empty milk crates. Sherona would reheat her food in the non-microwave-safe Tupperware. She would serve Dad first, then me, then herself. If she were feeling generous, she would offer some to Ali. Jean-Guy and Paul stuck to junk food they brought themselves.

Late in the night, as fatigue took over, I would see the outlines of Sherona, Ali, Jean-Guy, and Paul floating behind them after they walked away from me. Even my own hands and the mop I was holding would become two or three images waving before my eyes. Those were the times I cursed Dad for ruining my summer by forcing me to come work with him. He couldn't understand why I would want to get a job at the Rideau Centre or babysitting some stranger's children when he needed me.

We usually worked in pairs, and I was usually paired up with Sherona or Dad. I sprayed and cleaned all the glass doors from top to bottom. I also had to clean the bathrooms. Crap and piss smattered the inside of the bowls and the underside of the toilet seats. One night we found crap smeared on one of the walls inside a men's bathroom stall. That night I was working with Dad. He wouldn't look at me, just stood there leaning on his mop and staring at the stall. I didn't know what would happen. I said, "Dad, it's okay. I don't mind cleaning it." He remained quiet for a few more seconds, then shook his head, and told me get started in the women's bathroom. I tried to argue, but he shooed me away.

He showed me how to mop the floors with the long woolly mops, by walking backwards with the mop in front of me, making steady sweeping gestures from left to right like an unsung amateur hockey hero. I would dip the mop into the hot soapy water, lift it carefully, twirl it into the metal wringer hanging off the side of the bucket, then push down the handle just enough to squeeze out the excess water. I would continue the process, sweeping the mop across the floor, dipping and wringing it out as needed, until I reached the end of each long hallway.

He taught me to use the buffer machine, touching the throttle lightly, like a motorcycle, in order to maintain a steady rhythm. I watched him mop and wax endless hallways, then after they had dried, buff them to a glass-like shine from one end to the other. I would follow him with a dry mop, wiping up the wet streaks left by the buffer. We didn't talk during this time. We were each in our own worlds.

His hands were always cracked and dry and his clothes smelled like liquid soap, but at the end of the night he would smile and pat me on the back. As the light of summer mornings filled the building's foyer, the heaviness of night lifted from my body. I often felt light-headed—mostly from sleep deprivation, but also from the disbelief that I'd actually made it through another night. Some of the workers were already coming in as we were preparing to leave. We held the heavy glass doors open as they brushed past us, takeout coffee in hand and a quick "thank you" or "merci" floating backwards. It was hard to believe that minutes earlier we were the only ones occupying the building.

I was always anxious to get home, grab a few hours of sleep, and try to squeeze some normalcy out of my summer. But in a few short hours, the phone would ring, and I would head downstairs to the corner of Chapel and Lees Avenue to wait for Dad to pick me up for another night cleaning the factory on the other side of the Ottawa River.

What Inspired Me to Write This Selection

> I wrote this piece after listening to a song about the struggles of poor black people (*Fast Cars* by Tracy Chapman). The song reminded me of my teen years, a time in my life when I didn't feel very hopeful and wasn't sure if things would get better for my family and me. Things didn't get much better for my family but with some support (and the help of writing) I eventually found a way out of the unhappiness. Writing this piece was a way to have a record of those struggles and an equally important record of my survival.

After

1. Reading for Meaning The author makes certain judgments on everyone in the cleaning crew, but her tone is not unkind. Complete

Name	Quotation	Author's Attitude

a chart that includes the name of each person on the cleaning crew, a quotation from this memoir that describes each person, and a short phrase to describe the author's underlying attitude toward that person.

2. Understanding Form and Style
   a) Describe the pace of this memoir.
   b) What words or techniques did the author use to create this pace?

3. Critical Literacy How does the author get us to both like and dislike her dad in this memoir?

4. Metacognition How did making personal connections to the author's relationship with her father help you understand her emotions and thoughts in this memoir?

Beyond

1. Student Voice The author says she was inspired to write this piece after listening to a song. Think of a song that has reminded you of your current situation or an experience in your past. Respond to the song with a short memoir, a journal entry, some photographs, or an illustration, and explain the connection.

2. Speaking and Listening Interview one of your parents or guardians, or another adult you know, about a memorable job he or she had as a teenager. Be sure to ask questions to try to understand the details of his or her experience and what he or she liked and disliked about the job. Afterwards, write a short summary of your interviewee's job experience and compare and contrast it with the author's experience.

Perspective

Autobiography

Written by Taren Orchard

Taren Orchard is a student at the University of Winnipeg. He was moved around a lot as a child, from different family members to different foster families. He has lived in Winnipeg, Manitoba, and various places in Ontario, including Kenora, Dalles Reserve, Red Lake, and Thunder Bay. He loves listening to music as well as writing and playing music. He is proudly Ojibwa.

Tips

residential schools: church-run boarding schools set up to educate First Nations, Inuit, and Métis children in Euro-Canadian culture, as well as to discourage the children's traditional customs, languages, and beliefs. Children were sometimes forcibly removed from their homes to live in schools far from their communities.

autobiography: an account of a person's life written by that person

inference: meaning reached by a reader based on what the author states or implies as well as the reader's prior knowledge or experience

Before

What do you think hope means? Think of a time in your life when you had hope. Did being hopeful help you or not?

During

Create a timeline from the author's birth to when he is eighteen years old. As you read, mark important events in the author's life on the timeline.

My name is Taren Orchard. I'm eighteen years old and am a first-year university student at the University of Winnipeg. I am of First Nations descent. In my short life I have been through a lot. There are good and bad events that have shaped me into what I am today. I am sharing my story with you in hopes you might learn something about yourself and that I could learn from myself as well.

Everyone has events that shape them, most of these events are generational and a person wouldn't even know about them. If your parents had done something differently, you would probably be a slightly different person. I've heard stories about my family's past from my father. He's told me about a lot of the hardships he's gone through. Our lives are similar, you see; we both were lost by our parents. I grew up not exactly knowing what I was racially, and I had no one to answer the millions of questions I had.

I was born in Winnipeg, Manitoba, on September 8, around noon or so. My mom's name is Doris Wiley and my father's name is Patrick Orchard. I have only a few memories about my early years, but my dad tells me that when I was a little guy I was as cute as a bear cub, so much so that he gave me the nickname "Little Bear." After seeing some pictures of me when I was young, I have to agree with my dad's assessment.

My first home was a trailer in a trailer park. I am not exactly sure where it was—it never really mattered to me where it was. I just knew I was happy there. In that trailer I got the first real injury I can remember. I was watching Barney on the television and I thought it would be a great idea to hug Barney through the set. Sadly, my plan backfired and the television fell on top of me. Now I think it's kind of sad that I resorted to hugging a TV. I think I just wanted someone to hold.

My dad was the lead singer in a mildly successful band and he was constantly on tour. My mother was usually out drinking or partying. I didn't know why she would go out for such a long time. I wanted her to be home for me and my family. One weekend my father was on tour and my mother decided to leave. She left us little ones to take care of one another. We hadn't even begun school yet. That was the first time we were apprehended by Child and Family Services.

After a while in a foster home, my grandmother applied for custody for us kids; she eventually got it. I was reunited with my baby sister. The happy times began again. We lived there for a while, going to school, doing small chores around the house, having fun playing video games. I had daily visits with my dad, but rarely with my mom. The only time I would see my mom was when she was acting all crazy or drunk. I remember one night she went off pretty bad and she tried to break into the house where my grandmother lived.

My dad and his new girlfriend, Reba, had a daughter and named her Kiara Faith. But soon my father was diagnosed with lung cancer and he gave my mother custody of us because he did not want us around during his treatment. Our mother, Doris, took us to Dalles Reserve outside Kenora to live for a while, and then she took us to Thunder Bay, Ontario. Doris then went out drinking.

The Dreamers by Jim Logan

She got us a babysitter who was only supposed to watch us for two hours. Doris left for three days, and the babysitter left in the afternoon of the second day. A day later Child and Family Services was there once again to take us away.

Eventually my father regained custody of us, and we moved back to Kenora. My auntie Della passed away just before we got there. My father once again could not quite take care of us or give us the attention we needed, so he made an arrangement with Doris to keep us for three months until everything was cleared up. We lived in Kenora and my dad moved to Winnipeg to settle things there. I thought things would be good; I thought I would finally have a normal life with parents who would always be there when I needed them. I was living with my one brother, Lane, and two sisters, Tia Rose and Brooklyn. About a month or two later, we were apprehended by Child and Family Services again. We were taken away from Kenora to Red Lake.

Being in foster care was fine, so long as I was with the right people. The family my brother and I lived with in Red Lake was really great. I still talk to them sometimes. Then I hear about stories other people would share—they would say the most horrible things about certain families. I doubted a lot of the stories were true. I didn't like how people would label foster families as bad people. Of all the homes I was in, only one was bad, and that was when I was a little guy.

The parents of the family in Red Lake were named Joe and Wendy. They had two of their own children and another foster kid; their names were Shelby, Braeton, and Bobby. We all got along pretty well, although we all did have our differences. One thing I didn't like about living there is that my sisters weren't able to join us. We would visit them once in a while, not a whole lot, just enough so that we could remember their faces, I guess.

When we were on Christmas break, it was colder than a dead person at the bottom of the sea. One night, my brother and I came home from hanging out with friends, and our foster parents had news for us. Our dad had won custody of us kids except for little Tia, who wasn't his child. On Boxing Day we would once be again living with our real father. I thought that this year couldn't possibly get any better.

On Christmas Day, Lane and I were awoken by Shelby, who said it was time to open presents. To our surprise, we had presents under the tree, too. That memory is one of my favourites. I think that's what makes me remember that family so well—how nice they were, what good parents they were. They never asked us to come back. I think one day I might just want to surprise them and show up. I haven't seen them since the morning we left. It saddens me to think that we were only a small chapter of their lives, yet they were so monumental to us.

After finishing elementary school in Winnipeg, I attended a middle school called General Wolfe, where I learned about First Nations heritage and old ways of life. I attended sweats and sacred ceremonies with the Boys' Sharing Circle Program. I finally found out who I really was, and I really liked it. I knew I wasn't a drunk, a druggie, or a lazy Indian, as some people have called me in my past. I knew from then on that I was an Ojibwa First Nations student and I had a lot I could do with my life. Suddenly my life became important to me.

My life has been short, but it has been full of experiences and events that I pray no others will go through, even though the journey has been life changing or life making for me. Most of all, I hope every Native person out there will refuse to let the legacy of residential schools shape their children. Residential schools were designed to "Kill the Indian in the child," since assimilation was near impossible. We need to forgive and forget, and that means that as a people we need to acknowledge what went on and the harm that was done. I might not have attended those schools and I sure as hell am not going to let some stereotype ruin my children's lives, but my dad's and my biological mother's lives were changed because their parents went to residential school and it changed the way they lived. We as First Nations people should remember the teachings of old, and we must rebuild all that was lost. It's no one else's fault. We're not children of the crown anymore—we are our own people.

Now I'm eighteen and I've graduated from high school. I play music, I write music, I listen to music. I'm still Aboriginal and nothing will change that. I'm very happy and nothing will change that. I'll never forget the really important things. I know I won't ever forget my younger years. I'll share my own stories, along with stories that were shared with me when I was younger. This is the start of a new generation for the Orchard family. It's going to be great!

What Inspired Me to Write This Selection

66 Originally, my piece was written for a class project on the impact of Indian residential schools. Of course, I'm too young to have experienced residential schools directly, so I decided to write out the story of my life. I felt it would be a good example of the inter-generational effects First Nations families could feel. I never thought I was any good at writing, but I tried to focus on telling my story in a way it could reach people. 99

A carpentry class at a residential school called Brandon Indian Industrial School, in Brandon, Manitoba. The photo was taken in approximately 1910.

After

1. **Understanding Form and Style**
   a) How can you tell by reading this selection that it is an autobiography?
   b) Do you think the author could have told his life story effectively in a different format, such as a poem, song, or series of photographs? Why or why not?

2. **Reading for Meaning**   Make inferences to explain why you think the author usually refers to his mother by her first name.

3. **Reading for Meaning**   In what ways does the author believe residential schools affected his life?

4. **Speaking and Listening**
   a) Team up in pairs. One person summarizes the author's life for the second person.
   b) The second person now interviews the summarizer to clarify any part of the story that was confusing or missing an important detail.
   c) Give each other feedback on your summarizing and interviewing skills.

5. **Student Voice**   The author states, "There are good and bad events that have shaped me into what I am today." Do you think bad events in a person's life can actually have a positive impact on the shaping of his or her identity? Why or why not?

6. **Critical Literacy**
   a) Identify the points in the author's life when he appears to have been happy. What seems to make him happy? What does this tell you about what is important to the author?
   b) Do you always believe the author when he says he was happy? Why or why not?

7. **Metacognition**   What did you learn about the autobiography genre that you might use if you were to write your own autobiography?

Beyond

Viewing and Representing   As a class, use your teacher's guidance to choose and view a documentary on the residential school system in Canada. How does the knowledge you gained from this documentary affect your understanding of this selection? Keep in mind that the author's grandparents went to residential schools.

Letters to High School Selves

Letter

Written by Jeff Francis and Lorne Cardinal

Tips

tone: the attitude that runs through an entire text. This may include the writer's attitude towards the subject and/or the audience.

diction: the choice of words or phrases in speech or writing

Before

These letters were written by a major-league baseball player and a successful actor to themselves as high school students. What kind of advice might these two famous people give to their high school selves?

During

As you read, make a Venn diagram to compare the two letters. Look for both similarities and differences.

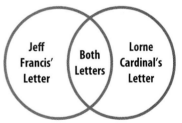

Jeff Francis' Letter — Both Letters — Lorne Cardinal's Letter

Written by Jeff Francis

Jeff Francis was born in Vancouver, British Columbia, and attended North Delta Senior Secondary School in North Delta. He was selected in the first round by the Colorado Rockies in the 2002 Major League Baseball draft. In his professional career, Jeff has lived all over the United States. He currently lives in Denver, Colorado, with his wife Allison, his daughter Cameron, and his son Miles.

Dear Jeff,

Hey it's me, you from the future. Twelve years in the future to be exact. The future is a good place, although not much different from where you are.

The Canucks still have not won a Stanley Cup, and although the Red Sox did eventually win a World Series, I still don't like them.

I'm not writing you to inform you of some big mistake you are to make later in life that changes you forever. In fact, life is pretty good; a beautiful wife, two unbelievable kids, a home (not telling where—it's a surprise!), and a career playing baseball in the Major Leagues. There's a lot to look forward to. However, don't think it's just going to happen. There is a lot of hard work and sacrifice that goes into achieving what you want (I know you know that already, just putting it here for effect).

As a Canadian playing professional baseball, you will be somewhat against the odds. As of now, out of almost 18 000 players who have played Major League baseball in more than 100 years, only 235 have been Canadian. As low as that is, I'd say it's fairly impressive given our country's obsession with hockey.

But what does it mean to be Canadian? There are so many different answers. We are known around the world to be overly nice and polite people, and for good reason. What other people on earth could suffer through the type of severe weather we do and yet still remain so optimistic and compassionate? With so many ethnic backgrounds in Canada, our identity can be hard to define with certainty.

Being Canadian is and should be a source of pride for anyone representing our country abroad, not just athletes. However, being Canadian means more than just being born there. As Canadians, we stand up for what we believe while respecting the views of others. We treat our neighbours the way we would want to be treated, and we often think of others before ourselves. This and much more makes us uniquely Canadian, and, in my opinion, the envy of the world.

Specifically, Canadian baseball players share a drive and work ethic that is not common among their peers. You can say it comes from our love of the game of hockey, or our blue-collar roots but, either way, Canadian baseball players play with a heart and passion that is, in my opinion, unmatched. You have this working on your side.

When you embark on your career in baseball, don't be preoccupied with fitting in. Embrace what makes you subtly different. I was always a little bit reluctant to be different from other people. Now I say wear your "Canadian-ness" on your sleeve. Instead of ordering a coffee in *tall, grande,* or *venti*, order a *double-double* just to see the looks on their faces. Go to a gas station and ask what the price is per litre. Ask everyone why their address has a zip code instead of a postal code. And *always*, say *zed*, not *zee*. It drives them bonkers.

Take my word for it; I wish I had been more aware of my Canadian-ness as a younger man. Here's a great quote from one of my favourite Canadian authors:

> I read and learned and fretted more about Canada after I left than I ever did while I was home. I absorbed anything I could on topics that ranged from folklore to history to political manifestos … I ranted and raved and seethed about things beyond my control. In short I acted like a Canadian. —Will Ferguson

Sincerely,

Jeff Francis pitching for the Colorado Rockies.

What Inspired Me to Write This Selection

" When I was asked to write a letter to myself as a teenager, I thought about all the things I would have done differently over the last fifteen years or so. But then I thought about how all those things have added up to create who I am now and where I stand. I guess there's not much I really would do differently. But one piece of advice I wish I had heard a little earlier in life was to really embrace what it means to be Canadian. When you live in Canada and nowhere else, it is hard to really know what that means, but after spending ten years in the United States, I realize what a special place Canada is and how proud we all should be of what we have at home. *"*

Written by Lorne Cardinal

Lorne is an actor and director best known for his roles on *Corner Gas* and *North of 60*. He's worked across the country and the United States for over twenty years in theatre, TV, radio, and film. While growing up, he lived in High Prairie, Ft. Vermillion, Prince George, Keremeos, Kamloops, Kelowna, and Edmonton. With the many moves came new schools. He and his brother were practised at being the new kids!

Dear Lorne,

Hey there, bud, in 1980. I hope your day's going good! You're probably anywhere except class, so on that note I thought I'd give you some advice from here in the future! I'd like to tell you stuff that would help the bank account, like buy Bre-X stock or Apple but I'll share a few things more valuable ...

First, stop skipping classes because you're only hurting yourself; you'll find that out when you try to get into college a little bit down the road and find that 50 percent average isn't what schools are looking for and you'll spend precious time having to upgrade. I know no one ever said it to you but, believe me, you're a heck of a lot smarter than you think, so put in the effort and you'll be surprised at how it pays off. Plus, you love English, social studies, history, biology, and the arts anyway!

Secondly, I can't stress how important it is to *be yourself*! Try not to worry about what others think about you. Just try to be honest and respectful to yourself and others. Try to look for important things in people, like integrity, honesty, and loyalty. Also, how people treat others is a good indicator of their spirit and how they'll most likely treat you!

Thirdly, try to listen to your dad. I know it's tough and he's in a bad place right at the moment, and you feel left alone to tend to things, but I'll tell you, he knows what he's talking about. It is important to understand your culture, and the history of your people and family because that's where your strength will come from when faced with adversity. Eventually things will be clear when you find out what he went through at residential school. It will explain his behaviour and the anger he has towards everybody at this time. Have patience and realize that he is doing the best he can with what he knows.

Lastly, tell him how much you love him, or, when it's safe, how much you're mad at him because he'll understand and talk to you about things ... Also, even though he hasn't said it and you haven't given him a lot to work with at this time, but he *is* proud of you and he loves you! This is important for you to know because when he's passed on, you will miss him every day and wish you could've said this more: I LOVE YOU, DAD!

Yours truly,

Lorne Cardinal

Lorne Cardinal playing Davis on the TV show *Corner Gas*.

What Inspired Me to Write This Selection

> ❝ I wanted to share some advice I wished I'd had in the tumultuous times when I was growing up. High school can be challenging and it's easy to forget that life is a long road beyond these years. You want to start practising positive attitudes and approaches to life as early as possible. I believe if you respect yourself and have faith in your skills and abilities, the respect of others will follow. As my father said, 'How can you love others if you don't love yourself first?' ❞

After

1. **Reading for Meaning**
   a) In two or three sentences, summarize the advice each author gives in his letter.
   b) How might you apply this advice in your own life?

2. **Understanding Form and Style**
   a) How might these two letters have been different if they were written as essays? Think about the tone, diction, and potential content that would be appropriate for this formal writing format.
   b) How might the differences you identified in part (a) change the effect the pieces have on the reader?

3. **Speaking and Listening** Review the Venn diagram you made for the During reading activity in which you outlined the similarities and differences between the two letters. Have a discussion with classmates about which letter had the greatest impact on you. As you are commenting, be aware of how your diction, tone, and facial expression convey extra meaning to the people listening to you.

4. **Student Voice** Both authors stress the importance of a strong work ethic. Often older generations see younger generations as not having a strong work ethic. Do you think your generation has a strong work ethic? Provide evidence for your answer.

5. **Critical Literacy** How might the effect of these letters be different if Jeff Francis was not a professional baseball player, and Lorne Francis was not a successful actor and director? Explain.

6. **Metacognition** How did summarizing the advice presented in these two letters affect your understanding of them?

Beyond

Student Voice Imagine yourself successful in the future. Following these authors' examples, write a letter or create a video of your future self speaking to your high school self.

Glossary

A

abbreviation: a shortened form of a word or phrase, such as *km/h* for kilometre per hour

allusion: a brief reference, explicit or implicit, to a place, person, or event

archetype: typical or perfect example of something; for example, "They are the *archetype* of a modern family."

autobiography: an account of a person's life written by that person

B

bias: show prejudice for or against something or someone

bullet point: a word or short phrase with a small printed symbol in front of it. Bullet points are often used in lists or to set apart important points in a larger piece of writing.

C

caricature: an illustration or description of a person or thing in which certain qualities are exaggerated to create a comic effect

climax: the most intense point in a plot, which involves a turning point in action

convention: a practice or device that is accepted as a necessary, useful, or given part of a genre

D

dialogue: conversation between two or more people in a story

diction: the choice of words or phrases in speech or writing

E

epilogue: a concluding section added to a literary work, such as a story, novel, or play

F

first-person narrative: a story told from the perspective of a character in the story as he or she experiences it. It can be identified by the use of the first-person pronoun *I*.

first-person point of view: the perspective of a character in the story as he or she experiences it. It can be identified by the use of the pronoun *I*.

flashback: a literary device in which the plot is interrupted by an event or incident from an earlier time; the story goes back in time

forward slash (/): a punctuation mark most commonly used as a substitute for the word *or*

G

genre: types or categories of literary work or entertainment recognized by form and/or style; for example, essay, article, short story, graphic novel, poem, science fiction novel, mystery novel

graffiti: writing or images painted onto public spaces

I

i.e.,: abbreviation for the Latin term *id est*, which means *that is* or *in other words*

imagery: the use of sensory details to evoke a mental picture. Imagery appeals to any of the five senses: sight, sound, taste, touch, or smell.

independent clause: a group of words that has both a subject and a verb and that could stand alone as a sentence

infer: to understand something based on what the author states or implies as well as your prior knowledge or experience; to conclude something based on facts and reasoning

inference: the meaning reached by a reader based on what the author states or implies as well as the reader's prior knowledge or experience

initialism: an abbreviation formed using the first letter or letters of each word in a phrase or name. For example, *AKA* is an initialism for *also known as*. Initialisms are often called acronyms, although an acronym should technically form a pronounceable word, such as the acronym *radar* for *radio detecting and ranging*.

L

literary devices: deliberate use of language to create a particular effect; for example, allusion, imagery, symbolism, metaphor, simile

M

matrix: a graphic representation of information that includes symbols, numbers, and text. A matrix has two lines that intersect in the middle. Opposite ideas, such as survival and death, appear at each end of each line.

memoir: an account of the personal experiences of an author

metaphor: a comparison between two objects or ideas without using the words *like* or *as*

mood: the atmosphere of a piece of writing that is meant to evoke a certain emotion or feeling from the reader

N

narrative box: a box in a panel of a graphic story that includes text that is not dialogue

P

pace: the speed at which an author tells a story

panel: a framed section of a graphic story

paraphrase: restating an idea or text using your own words

portrait: a likeness of a person, particularly showing the face, created by an artist or photographer

profile: a short biographical text presenting a person's most noteworthy characteristics and achievements

prologue: an introduction to a literary work, such as a play, autobiography, or novel

proposal: a plan or suggestion put forward for consideration or discussion by others

Q

quotation: a passage of text or speech that is repeated by someone other than the original author or speaker

quotation marks (" "): punctuation used at the beginning and end of a direct quotation

R

rhetorical question: a question to which no answer is expected

rhyme scheme: the pattern of rhymes in a poem

S

scenario: an outline or model of an imagined sequence of events

self-portrait: a portrait an artist has created of him- or herself

semicolon (;): used to connect independent clauses, and suggest a closer relationship between the clauses than a period does

sentence fragment: often looks like a sentence, but does not contain a complete thought because either the subject or predicate is missing or incomplete

simile: a comparison made using the words *like* or *as*

speech bubble: a shape drawn around dialogue with a pointer towards the speaker in a graphic story

spoken word: a form of poetry recited to an audience. These poems often comment on current social issues and are told from the first-person perspective.

stanza: a grouping of lines in a poem, set off by a space

symbol: one thing that stands for another, as in a flag representing a country

symbolic: representing something using symbols

symbolism: the use of symbols to represent ideas or emotions

T

third-person point of view: the perspective of the narrator, who is not a character in the story

tone: the attitude that runs through an entire text. This may include the writer's attitude towards the subject and/or the audience.

V

vocal inflection: change in the tone, pitch, or volume of a person's voice

voice: conveys the attitude, tone, and thought patterns of the narrator or speaker in writing

Photo and Art Credits

Section 1: Visual Forms

pp. 2–3: © PA Photos Limited/CP Images; p. 4: Courtesy of the author; pp. 5–8, 10: © Steven Keewatin Sanderson; p. 12: Courtesy of the authors; p. 13: photo by Stephen Morton; p. 14: (top) © Jessie Huggard, (bottom) © Megan Potts; p. 15: (top) © Brooke Carey, (bottom) © Courtney Morey; p. 17: © Jonni Super; pp. 18–23: © Claudia Dávila; p. 25: Courtesy of the authors; p. 26: © Karmen Fofana; p. 27: © David Clifton; p. 28: © Gabby Krizan; p. 30: Courtesy of the author; p. 31: © Kenneth Sutherland; p. 33: © Nadirah Zakariya; p. 34: © Jillian Tamaki; p. 39: Courtesy of the author; pp. 40–44: © Joe Ollmann.

Section 2: Fiction and Poetry

p. 47: © Artwork by Su Blackwell, photograph by Johanna Parkin; p. 48: Courtesy of the author; p. 49: © Gunter Marx/BC/Alamy; p. 51: © Don Denton/CP Images; p. 53: © Jing-Ling Kao-Beserve; pp. 54–55, 57: Michelle Woodward; p. 60: Courtesy of the author; p. 61: © Matt Rainey/Star Ledger/ Corbis; p. 62: © Sergey Vasilyev/Shutterstock; p. 65: Courtesy of the author; pp. 67–68: Joey Marsh/ Shannon Associates; p. 70: © Michael Galan; pp. 72, 74: © Jan Feindt/Gerald & Cullen Rapp; p. 76: Courtesy of the authors; p. 77: © Purestock/SuperStock/Laserwords; p. 79: © Patrizia Tilly/Shutterstock/ Laserwords; p. 80: © Triff/Shutterstock/Laserwords.

Section 3: Forms of Nonfiction

p. 83: © Elton Fernandes; p. 84: Courtesy of the authors; p. 85: © Dr. Scott T. Grafton/Visuals Unlimited; p. 87: © Darryl Dyck/CP Images; p. 89: © Gianni Dagli Orti/Corbis; p. 91: © C.J Lafrance/ZUMA Press/ Corbis; p. 93: Courtesy of the author; p. 94: (top) © Gamma-Rapho/Getty Images, (bottom) © Mike Deal/Winnipeg Free Press/AP Photo; p. 95: © Jason Merritt/FilmMagic/Getty Images; p. 96: © Michael Ochs Archives/Getty Images; p. 97: © INFevents.com/CP Images; p. 99: Courtesy of the author; p. 100: © Michelle Verbeek Photography; p. 102: © Tracy O'Camera Photography; p. 104: Courtesy of the author; p. 105: © Max Earey/Shutterstock; p. 106: © Qi Heng/Xinhua Press/Corbis; p. 108: Courtesy of the author; p. 109: © James Egan Photography; p. 111: Courtesy of Carol Huynh; p. 113: © Marty Lederhandler/AP Photo/CP Images; p. 116: Courtesy of the author; p. 117: © Norm LeBus Photo; p. 118: © Katie Gad; p. 120: © Kerstin Joensson/AP Photo/CP Images.

Section 4: Memoirs and Personal Reflections

pp. 122–123: © Cynthia Sheppard; p. 124: Courtesy of the author; p. 125: © Vico Collective/Alin Dragulin/Blend Images/Getty Images/Laserwords; p. 126: © Robyn Mackenzie/Shutterstock/Laserwords; p. 128: © numb/Alamy/Laserwords; p. 130: © Melissa Zimmermann; p. 131: © Radius Images/Getty Images; p. 134: © Paul Zemokhol; p. 136: © Adri Berger/Getty Images; p. 137: © Jupiterimages/ Getty Images; p. 139: Courtesy of the author; p. 141: © Jim Logan; p. 143: UCCA, 93.049P/1368N/A carpentry class at the Brandon Indian Industrial School, Brandon, Manitoba, ca 1910; p. 145: (left) Courtesy of the author, (right) © Alan Fiedel; p. 147: Courtesy of the author; p. 149: © Alan Fiedel.

Text Credits

All selections used with permission of the authors.